"I love a book that is both practical and cor____ than a biblical approach to our emotions! V____ women walk us through the process of identifying our feelings, and then they show us how to profit from and guide them in a God-glorifying way."

Nancy Wilson, pastor's wife; homemaker; grandmother of seventeen; author, *Learning Contentment*

"This gifted mother-and-daughter team do it again! With striking clarity, insightful illustrations, and the wisdom that comes from walking with God, Carolyn and Nicole put to rest the ever-ready excuse, 'I just can't help how I feel.' They teach us from Scripture why God gave us emotions and how to interpret what those emotions reveal about our actual beliefs and values. For anyone who has ever felt confused, guilty, or exhausted by runaway emotions, *True Feelings* is a must read."

Jani Ortlund, speaker, Renewal Ministries; author, *Fearlessly Feminine* and *His Loving Law, Our Lasting Legacy*

"The best books are well-written, biblically sound, have universal appeal, and offer both penetrating insight and practical help. The mother/daughter writing team of Carolyn Mahaney and Nicole Whitacre has given us such a book. Women are their primary audience, but nearly all the book is applicable to men. They'll surprise you by showing how often the Bible speaks to the subject of emotions and thereby help you see fresh insights into familiar texts. Carolyn and Nicole are honest about the reality of negative feelings and avoid the simplistic, shallow, 'turn lemons into lemonade' answers. Emotions are a God-created part of each of us. They tell us what we value and move us to action. But like every other part of us they are affected by sin, yet can be sanctified for our joy and God's glory. As every Christian can identify with this struggle, so every Christian can benefit from this book."

Donald S. and Caffy Whitney, professor of biblical spirituality and associate dean, School of Theology, The Southern Baptist Theological Seminary; author, *Family Worship*; and his wife, Caffy

"*True Feelings* is an excellent book about the goodness and grace of God in the middle of our many emotions. Carolyn and Nicole consistently point us to God's Word, and practical wisdom flows from every page. Read this book, and be reminded that the Lord alone is our help and hope, regardless of our circumstances."

David and Heather Platt, president, International Mission Board; author, *Radical*; and his wife, Heather

"What do we do with our feelings? Jesus demands that every facet of our life be brought into submission to his lordship, even our emotions. Yet few Christians think about just how significant our emotions are in our daily lives. *True Feelings* is a needed resource that is biblically sound and theologically faithful. Carolyn Mahaney and Nicole Whitacre are sure guides for thinking biblically about our emotions as gifts of God needing redemption by the gospel of Jesus Christ."

R. Albert Mohler Jr. and Mary Mohler, president, The Southern Baptist Theological Seminary; and his wife, Mary, director, Seminary Wives Institute, The Southern Baptist Theological Seminary

"Through their careful research and engaging style, Carolyn and Nicole will leave you glad that God has given us emotions, less afraid of the more painful ones, more able to listen to what emotions are saying, and expectant that they can be refined and sanctified."

Ed Welch, counselor; faculty member, The Christian Counseling & Educational Foundation; author, *Shame Interrupted* and *Side by Side*

True Feelings

True Feelings

God's Gracious and Glorious
Purpose for Our Emotions

CAROLYN MAHANEY AND
NICOLE WHITACRE

WHEATON, ILLINOIS

True Feelings: God's Gracious and Glorious Purpose for Our Emotions

Copyright © 2017 by Carolyn Mahaney and Nicole Whitacre

Published by Crossway
        1300 Crescent Street
        Wheaton, Illinois 60187

Cover design: Crystal Courtney

First printing 2017

Printed in the United States of America

Unless otherwise indicated, Scripture quotations are from the ESV® Bible (The Holy Bible, English Standard Version®), copyright © 2001 by Crossway, a publishing ministry of Good News Publishers. Used by permission. All rights reserved.

Scripture references marked NIV are taken from The Holy Bible, New International Version®, NIV®. Copyright © 1973, 1978, 1984, 2011 by Biblica, Inc.™ Used by permission. All rights reserved worldwide.

All emphases in Scripture quotations have been added by the authors.

Trade paperback ISBN: 978-1-4335-5247-2
ePub ISBN: 978-1-4335-5250-2
PDF ISBN: 978-1-4335-5248-9
Mobipocket ISBN: 978-1-4335-5249-6

Library of Congress Cataloging-in-Publication Data

Names: Mahaney, Carolyn, 1955– author.
Title: True feelings : God's gracious and glorious purpose for our emotions / Carolyn Mahaney and Nicole Whitacre.
Description: Wheaton : Crossway, 2017. | Includes bibliographical references and index.
Identifiers: LCCN 2016049760 (print) | LCCN 2017009547 (ebook) | ISBN 9781433552472 (tp) | ISBN 9781433552489 (pdf) | ISBN 9781433552496 (mobi) | ISBN 9781433552502 (epub)
Subjects: LCSH: Emotions—Religious aspects—Christianity.
Classification: LCC BV4597.3 .M34 2017 (print) | LCC BV4597.3 (ebook) | DDC 248.4—dc23
LC record available at https://lccn.loc.gov/2016049760

Crossway is a publishing ministry of Good News Publishers.

LB   27   26   25   24   23   22   21   20   19   18   17
15   14   13   12   11   10   9   8   7   6   5   4   3   2

To the girlies—Caly, Tori, MJ, Sophie, Claire, and Summer

Contents

Foreword

Every woman loves . . . and despises them.

I'm talking about emotions. When your feelings rise to euphoric delight, your heart longs to live there, like: *This is me, the true me . . . this is who God destined me to be.* The next day, a burnt casserole, broken dishwasher, and a stubbed toe have you feeling depressed and fuming: *Yep, this is me, the true me . . . this is who God destined me to be, an emotional basket case: happy one day, crashing the next.*

But before you cry, "Oh God, who will rescue me from this body of sin and death?" (Paul's words, not mine), remember this: Christ died for *all* of you, not just your body and spirit, but your emotions too. God is into redeeming everything about you, even your fluctuating feelings. And as a follower of Jesus, you have the glad-hearted assistance of the Holy Spirit in taming them.

Need help? Sure, you do. And this is why I am glad you have *True Feelings: God's Gracious and Glorious Purpose for Our Emotions.* My friend Carolyn Mahaney, with the aid of her daughter Nicole Whitacre, writes a compelling and glorious guide for every woman seeking to understand her emotions from God's point of view. And not only understand, but subdue and even appreciate them.

In Carolyn and Nicole, you will find two trusted friends. Seasoned Christians who understand emotional upheavals and deep disappointments, they have a true heart to help other women move forward into Christ-honoring maturity. Carolyn and Nicole know that your emotions have to come along on that ride . . . and thus, the reason for this book.

If you want your feelings to conform to the Lord and Savior who utterly delights in you, whose emotions overflow for you, then you will find a worthy guide and companion in *True Feelings*. So get started, turn the page, and be blessed by Carolyn Mahaney and Nicole Whitacre's wise reflections. I have a *feeling* you are going to like this book!

Joni Eareckson Tada
Joni and Friends International Disability Center
Agoura Hills, California

The Soaring Pays for the Thud ... Or Does It?

John Calvin Layman was not a man in touch with his feelings. Each day he woke his sons before dawn and strode ahead of them to the barn where forty cows were stomping and snorting in the frigid air waiting to be milked. If his boys didn't feel like coming out from under the warm covers, they would feel a whole lot worse five minutes later when their father poured a bucket of cold water on them in their bed. John Calvin Layman never said anything twice.

Our esteemed ancestor, John Calvin Layman, was a Mennonite dairy farmer in rural Virginia. A short, solid, serious man of Swiss-German stock, he had ten children, of whom Carolyn's father, Ezra, was the seventh. In many ways, Ezra grew up to be like his father. He rose every day at four and drove a company truck to his job as a construction superintendent.

He took his family to church twice on Sunday and every Wednesday evening. Ezra was gentle and hardworking, a man of strong, quiet conviction. He wasn't what you would call emotional. Neither is Carolyn.

You can imagine her culture shock when she joined her husband's gregarious Irish family in the Maryland suburbs. They were passionate and talkative, the men cried as often as the women (if not more!), and they all went into full-blown mourning every time their beloved Washington Redskins lost to the Dallas Cowboys.

Sometimes Carolyn wondered how to access the emotional world of her expressive preacher husband. She watched CJ worship and weep, wishing that she could feel the same joy and enthusiasm. She even felt guilty at times for not feeling as passionate for God as he seemed to. Even-keeled Carolyn and her loud, humorous husband had three daughters in quick succession: Nicole, Kristin, and Janelle; a son, Chad, was born twelve years later. Nicole, the oldest, inherited her emotional makeup from her father's side of the family, her personality bearing little resemblance to her Layman ancestors.

Once, when Nicole was sixteen years old, she traveled to India on a short-term mission trip. It was a three-week adrenaline rush. The team touched down in the sweltering city of New Delhi and boarded a train for the twenty-hour trip to the southern city of Hyderabad. Nicole bunked in a beautiful stone monastery, gained five pounds eating piles of delicious naan bread and potatoes, and was fitted for a bright green and saffron-colored sari by a local seamstress. She even walked the white marble floors of the Taj Mahal. Nicole's group visited villages and town squares doing open-air evangelism, and she had the privilege of praying with people to receive Christ. She felt exhilarated, inspired, and fulfilled. This was the life, and this was how she always wanted to feel.

Then she came home to her cookie-cutter house in the suburbs, to long afternoons as a church receptionist, and to six more weeks of summer where the most exciting event was the free-swim hour at the local pool. She was restless, discontent, and irritable. She wanted to feel those exhilarating feelings again as soon as possible. Nicole has always lived life at full throttle; her emotional switch came set on high. Whatever she feels, she feels it strongly.

As a mother and daughter, we share the same curve of mouth and slight stature, but we're different emotional creatures. Our differences are mirrored by an exchange between the fictional mother and daughter, Marilla Cuthbert and Anne Shirley, in the book *Anne of Avonlea*. Marilla says to her adopted daughter, Anne:

> "It seems to me, Anne, that you are never going to outgrow your fashion of setting your heart so on things and then crashing down into despair because you don't get them."
>
> "I know I'm much too inclined that way," agreed Anne ruefully. "When I think something nice is going to happen I seem to fly right up on the wings of anticipation; and then the first thing I realize I drop down to earth with a thud. But really, Marilla, the flying part *is* glorious as long as it lasts . . . it's like soaring through a sunset. I think it almost pays for the thud."

"Well, maybe it does," admitted Marilla. "I'd rather walk calmly along and do without both flying and thud."[1]

Walking calmly along, like Marilla, is what Laymans have done for generations, Carolyn not excepting. Nicole is like a blond-haired Anne, flying up on wings of anticipation and then crashing down into despair. Imagine Marilla Cuthbert and Anne Shirley writing a book together, and that'll give you an idea of what's ahead.

But that's only half the story. We may be emotional opposites, but we share a common curiosity and enthusiasm to learn what the Bible has to say about a woman's feelings.[2] Over the past couple of decades, we have studied God's Word and as many biblical resources as we could find on the complex topic of emotions. Whatever wisdom you find in these pages, we first learned from someone else. But we do have a lot of personal experience with emotions. Carolyn raised three daughters— a household full of hormones. They are all married now, and Nicole has two of the six granddaughters in the family. Our lives are fairly spilling over with feelings.

This is a book we wrote for ourselves as well as for the women and girls in our family whom we love. We also wrote this book for you. It's been an emotional journey. These pages echo with our laughter and are wet with more than a few of our tears. It has also been a surprising journey of learning about God's gracious and glorious purpose for our emotions. Our simple prayer is that every woman who reads this book will be surprised and delighted by how God created her to feel.

1

Fact, Fiction, and Feelings

Carolyn grew up near the shores of Lido Beach on the Gulf Coast of Florida. Here the white sand sparkles like quartz, pearly-pink coquinas dot the beach, and turquoise waves gently lap the shore. But powerful rip currents sometimes lurk beneath the tranquil waters. These narrow bands of swiftly moving water can pull even the strongest swimmer away from shore and out to sea. Rip currents pop up without warning, move at a breathtaking pace, and sap the strength of any swimmer who panics and tries to swim straight to shore. Tragically, many people lose their lives to these dangerous currents every year.

Carolyn remembers her mom, a perpetual worrier, warning her children before they went to the beach: "Whatever you do, watch out for rip currents!" The kids learned to be vigilant after a storm and especially careful when they swam out to a sandbar. One year, two friends from Canada, a brother and sister, came to visit and spend time at the beach. They were floating on their rafts when they drifted into one of these rip currents. Carolyn and her siblings watched, horrified, as the two friends tried to paddle back to shore, but the current took them farther and farther out to sea. Thankfully, one of the lifeguards on duty swam out to rescue Carolyn's frightened and exhausted friends. This experience lent new solemnity to her mother's warnings.

Our emotions can feel like an ocean full of rip currents. We're floating along on a sea of happy feelings when suddenly we get caught in a powerful current of anxiety, a fast-moving river of anger, or an unforeseen tide of depression. One moment we feel fine, and the next moment we are overwhelmed by hurt and bitterness, or we are jealous and upset. Your husband makes a comment. A friend shows off her ring. The toddler pours his milk all over the floor. A song replays your sadness. *Instantaneously. All of a sudden. Out of the blue.*

Emotional rip currents pull us into a whirlpool of confusion. "My emotions have extreme ups and downs," one college student wrote to us. "The hardest thing for me is understanding why they're there. Is it just hormones? Is it just because I'm tired? Is it the Devil attacking me? Or is it a reflection of how far away from God I am? Does it even matter where the feelings are coming from? It's so confusing." The questions come so fast that we can't keep pace. We worry that our fluctuating emotions mean that we are not trusting God or that we must be sinning in some way. Even those of us who aren't very emotional can wonder if something is wrong with us. We can't figure out why we feel (or don't feel) the way we do or what God wants us to do with our feelings—and so confusion leads to condemnation.

Feelings can be so unpleasant that at times we would rather do without them altogether. Gloomy feelings follow us around like Eeyore's cloud. Guilty feelings from the past won't leave us alone. We can't even feel happy in the present without worrying that something bad is going to happen in the future. And when something bad does happen, our emotions only make it worse. Not to mention that everyone else seems happy, and this makes us more miserable. Social media reinforces this perception: "Facebook is a constant bombardment of everyone else's great news," observed the author of a recent study, "but many of us look out of the window and see grey skies and rain. . . . This makes the Facebook world, where everyone's showing their best side, seem even more distortedly bright by contrast."[1] On social media, television, and even at church on Sundays, everyone appears to be happy. Everyone, that is, except for us. We take this distorted perception of reality and assume we should be feeling happy all the time too. But we don't, and so we feel even more depressed.

Many of us bury our unhappy emotions, keep a tight lid on them, stuff them deep down inside. Others of us explode and vent. Bad feelings lead to hasty reactions and poor decisions—which only brew more bad feelings of frustration, failure, shame, and regret. We make a mess of things because we feel bad, and then we feel bad because we made a mess of things. Another young woman wrote to tell us about her trouble with her feelings: "I get so discouraged when, for an ungodly and completely ridiculous reason, I get frustrated or very sad. These feelings immediately intensify as I am even more upset by the mere fact that I am feeling them. It's stupid, irrational, and so far from the holiness and Christlikeness that I desire. I never wanted to act like this—like a teenager. I feel utterly ridiculous."

I never wanted to act like this—like a hormonal teenager or an angry mom or a needy wife or an emotional woman. We all want to act mature, but our emotions often trip us up, sending us to the back of the godliness line. Not to mention that our feelings can sometimes make things awkward. The men in our lives don't seem to understand us, and we worry about showing too much emotion. We're embarrassed to laugh too loudly or cry at the wrong time. We don't want to be viewed as weak or vulnerable, but we feel powerless to resist the emotional rip currents in our lives. We don't know where they come from, when they will surface, or how to control them. We panic. We paddle. We drift into despair as the shoreline of serenity recedes into the distance.

Feelings feel bad. They feel unpredictable, confusing, and difficult to control. As Martyn Lloyd-Jones, a medical doctor and a pastor, famously put it, "I suppose that one of the greatest problems in our life . . . is the right handling of our feelings and emotions. Oh, the havoc that is wrought and the tragedy, the misery and the wretchedness that are to be found in the world simply because people do not know how to handle their own feelings!"[2] The good doctor was right. Emotional rip currents are one of the biggest problems in the Christian life.

A Sisterhood of Struggle

We all share in a sisterhood of struggle with our emotions. "No temptation has overtaken you that is not common to man" (1 Cor. 10:13). This verse offers solace to each of us when it comes to our feelings. Our temptations are *common*. Charles Spurgeon, a famous nineteenth-century pastor who wrestled with depression, wrote:

> I know that you are tempted to think that you are a lone traveler on a road and that nobody has ever traversed before you; but if you carefully examine the track, you can discover the footprints of some of the best of God's servants who have passed along that wearisome way. It is a very dark lane, you say—one that might truly be called, "Cut-throat Lane." Ah! but you will find that apostles have been along that way . . . martyrs have been that way, and the best of God's saints have been tempted just as you now are.[3]

"The best of God's saints" have traveled the rough road of emotions. You are not unique. You are not alone.

Knowing that we are not alone can help. We find comfort in connecting with someone who "gets" us, who feels the same way we do. How much more comforting is it that the men and women of Scripture and church history felt the same as us, not to mention countless Christians all over the world today? If we could talk to them, face-to-face, they would surely exclaim, "I

21

know what you mean!" and "I feel the same way!" Every feeling you have ever experienced has been felt by countless other Christians, many of whom were pillars of the faith.

In the process of writing this book, the women in our family—mother, daughters, and granddaughters—attended the public memorial service for the well-known missionary and author, Elisabeth Elliot, whose first husband, Jim Elliot, was killed by the Auca Indians. Toward the end of the beautiful and God-glorifying service, Valerie Shephard, Elisabeth Elliot's daughter, read excerpts from Elisabeth's jungle diary. One entry finds her lamenting her weaknesses and failures:

> Lack of patience with the Indians. Laziness in myself. Failure to discipline myself.

The next day she experiences a rip current of grief:

> The hours of early morning are always hardest for me for some reason. Perhaps because that is the time I always counted on to lie on Jim's strong shoulder. To wake and find his place empty beside me is a stab in the heart.

Another entry records her ongoing struggles:

> It has been hard today. I got so discouraged and impatient with these girls in school that I had to come downstairs for awhile and write a letter just for a break . . . I feel so helpless without Jim . . . O Lord help me, for I am truly helpless.[4]

Sound familiar? Like something you might write in your journal? Here was a widow and missionary, lying in a hammock in the jungles of Ecuador more than half a century ago, struggling with the same feelings of grief, loneliness, impatience, and discouragement we experience on a daily basis. How comforting that this godly woman was a woman like us.

But Elisabeth Elliot's difficult emotions did not have the last word. At her memorial service, friends and family shared stories of a woman who was full of life, joy, wonder, humor, and a peaceful acceptance of the will of God. Our heavenly Father helped Elisabeth Elliot to handle her emotions, and he will help us too.

What Plato Got Wrong

When we go looking for a solution to our emotional problems, however, we don't always open our Bibles. We think we'll feel condemned for our messy emotions, so we hold off until we feel better. Or, we assume that God cares only about what we do, not how we feel. But the opposite is true: God cares about our feelings—a whole lot more than we may realize. And did you know that the Bible tells us *how* to handle our emotions? Scripture isn't a dry, dull book; it is heavy with emotion and full of emotional stories. It speaks to feelings, and it speaks with feeling. As professor Sam Williams writes, "God's written Word is anything but silent about emotion."[5]

But as Christians, we often get mixed messages and contradictory advice about our feelings. "Throughout my Christian life I've been taught such differing views on emotions," one woman complained, "from 'just ignore your emotions completely' to 'you really need to work hard on changing your emotions.' As someone who is very open with my emotions and struggles with being governed by emotions, these differing views and the general lack of teaching on this topic make the struggle even harder." Confusion over our feelings spawns new rip currents of frustration, discouragement, and self-reproach, while so-called Christian advice only exacerbates our struggles.

Have you ever followed someone's advice and then discovered it was based on a myth? You know the type: "If you go swimming within thirty minutes after eating, you will get a cramp and drown" or "If you swallow chewing gum, it will stay in your stomach for seven years" or "If you go outside with wet hair, you will catch a cold." Many of us have spent years following these maxims only to discover they aren't true. As it turns out, many of us have also believed certain myths about what the Bible says regarding our feelings.

As the two of us have studied emotions over the years, we've been surprised to discover that a lot of commonly accepted truisms about emotions actually have pagan roots instead of a biblical foundation. Plato and the Stoics—not Scripture—promoted the idea that emotions are unruly, irrational, the enemy of virtue, and the weakest part of us. These philosophers believed that the mind and will are vastly superior and should rule over the emotions. Sadly, much of today's popular wisdom about emotions is rooted in this ancient tradition. Even some of the "wisdom" that gets passed around in Christian circles owes more to Stoic philosophy than biblical theology.

Many of us have unknowingly imbibed a lot of these

misconceptions about our feelings. We believe things like, "feelings are fickle" and "feelings are unreliable" and "don't trust your feelings." We contrast feelings with faith as if they were diametrically opposed to each other. And we assume "I can't help the way that I feel." We think and talk about emotions as if they are bad rather than good. But none of these "truths" about our feelings are true. So let's dispel a few myths: just as you won't carry around a wad of Juicy Fruit in your stomach for seven years, so your emotions are not bad, fickle, or uncontrollable.

The myths and misconceptions that cause much of our emotional confusion also lead to bad methods for handling our emotions. This, in turn, stunts our spiritual growth. Pastor Brian Borgman writes, "Why is it that people who attend good Bible-teaching churches with sound doctrine often fail to progress [in the Christian life], even though well-taught? . . . I propose that one of the reasons is that we do not have a biblical understanding of emotions, and therefore there is little or no biblical handling of the emotions."[6] We must return to what the Bible has to say about our emotions if we want to grow in godliness.

When we clear away the clutter of misconceptions and take another look at what Scripture teaches, we will unearth some wonderful truths about our feelings. We can change the way we feel! Scripture shows us that emotions are not unreliable, but are one of the most reliable things about us. Emotions are not a hindrance to wise decision making, but are central to the Christian life. Feelings are not bad. Instead, they play a good and useful role with the other faculties. God's Word doesn't pit feelings and truth against each other but calls us to feel more deeply about the things that are true. In other words, Scripture leads us to have *true feelings*.

The Solution from Scripture

Due to the range and complexity of human emotions, many aspects of emotions are beyond the scope of this book or our ability to address. We're not medical doctors or psychologists. We're one mother and one daughter, and we know enough to know how much we don't know. While this book is a short take on the expansive topic of feelings, we pray it will encourage you to bring all your emotional questions and troubles to Scripture. If you are experiencing an emotional crisis or extended emotional suffering, we do not come to force the light of truth down the tunnel of your soul; we simply want to talk to you, friend to friend, with all the love and limits that come with that relationship. If your situation warrants it, we urge you to seek pastoral counsel and, if necessary, medical advice. But this we know: no person or problem is beyond the reach of God's grace.

Whatever our emotional struggle—and we should put every confusing, bizarre, and unruly feeling in this category, leaving nothing out—we will find help and hope in the Bible. There is hope for the teenage girl who wonders why her emotions feel out of control and hope for the woman whose hormones stalk her every month. There is hope for the employee trying to manage stress in the workplace and for the mom who hates that she's always getting angry at her kids. There is hope for the middle-aged woman whose emotions have been scrambled by menopause and hope for the woman who feels locked in a dungeon of depression. There is hope for *every* woman "through the encouragement of the Scriptures" (Rom. 15:4).

Scripture's encouragement does not get rid of all of our unpleasant emotions; rather, it shows us that God has a purpose for our feelings—the good and the bad. Most of all, it proclaims the good news of the gospel: "For the grace of God has appeared, bringing salvation for all people" (Titus 2:11). God sent his Son to save us from our sins. Jesus Christ laid down his life for us, taking our place on the cross. He absorbed the wrath of God we so justly deserved. If God gave his Son for our sins, how much more will he help us to deal with the problem of our feelings!

When we lose heart, when we feel helpless to change our emotions, we must remember the gospel. God, who did not spare his own Son to save us from our sins (Rom. 8:32), will not leave us to drown in our emotional rip currents. There is no feeling too strong from which he cannot save. There is no person who has drifted too far that he cannot reach. The Lifeguard of our souls has come, and he will rescue us.

2

The Gift of Emotions

One Valentine's Day when Nicole and her sisters were little, Carolyn bought a bag of candy hearts—you know, the chalky pastel ones that say "Be mine" and "Love you"—and hid them in places CJ would be sure to find them: his winter gloves, his brown leather briefcase, and among the pens and paper clips of his desk drawer. She thought it would bring a smile to his face to see unexpected reminders throughout the day of how much she loved him. But when they sat down to dinner that night, CJ asked Carolyn, "Did the girls get a hold of a bag of Valentine's candy? I've been finding them everywhere!" When she explained that they were an "I love you" message from her, he replied, "I wish I would have known they were from you! I would have savored every single piece of candy knowing it was an expression of your love for me." When CJ thought the Valentine's candies were a mess made by his little girls, he tossed them out with hardly a second thought. If he had realized they were a gift from his loving wife, he would have appreciated them and been blessed by her thoughtfulness. Knowing who the giver is makes all the difference in how we receive the gift.

So it is with our emotions. We tend to view them as a nuisance and a problem, like chalky candies cluttering our lives. We don't know where they come from or what they're good for. They only seem to get in the way and mess things up. But did you know that our emotions are a gift *from God*? He gave them to us as an expression of his love. When we realize who gave us feelings, our view of emotions will change. Knowing that God is the giver makes all the difference in how we receive the gift of our emotions.

Because emotions are from God, they are a *good* gift. He embedded emotions in our humanity to serve a useful purpose in our lives. When God surveyed his creation and called it "good," he didn't mutter under his breath, "except for emotions!" No. God surveyed *everything* he had created and declared it all "very good," including our emotions (Gen. 1:31).

We appreciate the gift of emotions even more when we see how Scripture's descriptions of God swell with emotional language. God the Father was "angered" at the Israelite's murmuring (Deut. 1:34) and "pleased" at Solomon's request for discernment (1 Kings 3:10). God will "rejoice over [his people] with gladness" (Zeph. 3:17) and is "grieved . . . to his heart" at the wickedness of man (Gen. 6:6). Jesus was "moved with pity" for the leper (Mark 1:41) and "wept" at the news of

Lazarus's death (John 11:35). The Savior saw the crowds and "had compassion for them" (Matt. 9:36). It is possible for us to "grieve the Holy Spirit" (Eph. 4:30). If God describes himself using emotional language, how can we be averse to seeing ourselves as emotional creatures? Emotions are a good and glorious gift to every man and woman created in the image of God.

And God created each one of us with a unique emotional design. No two people *feel* alike. As women, we are not more emotional than men (try telling that to the men in your life!), for we are all emotional creatures. But God made men and women with unique emotional capacities; we feel and express our emotions in different ways, and thus men often find our emotions mysterious—and we don't always understand how they feel. As women, we have a greater capacity for certain emotions that correspond to our God-given design. Our emotional palettes have different shades and tones, giving us an emotional beauty and strength that is different from men but complementary to them as well. Mothers and daughters, sisters and friends, we are a beautiful, complex mosaic of emotions.

Splashing Color on the Canvas of Life

"Our emotions are our first response to the world around us," writes counselor Ed Welch.[1] Whether it's a surprise birthday party or a flat tire, a first date or an ordinary day, emotions react: we feel sad or happy, disappointed or scared, angry or hopeful. "What pain is to the nerve endings, what sweetness is to the taste buds, what light is to the eye, the feelings are to the soul."[2] And emotions propel us into relationships and adventure. When we feel compassion, we reach out and give someone a hug. When we feel happy, we smile and laugh. When we feel exuberant, we clap and cheer. Emotions play an integral role in our lives, from our relationships with God and others, to our memories, imaginations, and life experiences.

God created our emotions to work in harmony with our other two most fundamental faculties: the mind and the will. Just as our minds enable us to think and our wills enable us to choose, so our emotions enable us to respond. Our faculties are designed to function together, "properly and proportionally," in balance with one another, to make us fully human.[3] God wants us to put our emotions to work in equal measure with our minds and our wills.

To appreciate the gift of emotions, imagine what life would be like if you could not feel. Imagine hanging out with friends, yet feeling no pleasure in their company, or saying yes to the man on bended knee but feeling no butterflies? What if you held your squalling newborn to your chest with no elation or heard the diagnosis "all clear" with no flood of relief? Without emotions you would find no comfort in a good book, a bubble bath, or a drive in the country. Emotions add pleasure, comfort, and richness to events and relationships. Emotions color our lives.

Even difficult emotions reflect reality and can move us to a better place. Feelings mirror the pain and suffering in our lives. Imagine losing a close friend or a beloved family member and feeling no grief or loss. What if you hurt someone you love but felt no remorse or shame? Imagine getting fired or failing a test and feeling no disappointment. It might sound nice to do without these painful feelings, but none of us can deny that emotions give meaning and depth to our lives. Often the emotions we most wish we could avoid propel us in a new and better direction.

So the next time you laugh at your child's antics or feel exhilarated when you reach a goal, when you stand at the graveside of a loved one or keep watch over the death of your dreams, you are experiencing the emotions that enrich our lives. Without emotions, life would be a colorless canvas, boring and bland.

Where Emotions Went Wrong

While we may agree that feelings enhance our lives, it can still be hard to think of them as a good gift. All we have to do is consider the emotions we have felt just today, and we likely frown on the suggestion that emotions are good. We see emotions as interrupting instead of benefiting our lives. More often than not, we identify emotions as rip currents rather than blessings.

If God gave us feelings as a good gift, how did they get so messed up? To understand what went wrong with emotions, we have to go back to the beginning—almost. We have to understand what happened after God created emotions and declared them "very good" (Gen. 1:31). You know the story. The snake came. Adam and Eve disobeyed God. Sin entered the world. Everything went wrong, including our emotions. Here is the start of all our emotional problems.

Before sin, the first couple had the best of emotions. They experienced sweet fellowship with God, delight in one another, and pleasure in the garden where they lived (Gen. 2:4–25). They had no unpleasant feelings of fear or shame (v. 25). Emotions were exactly as God intended them to be. But all that changed when they ate the forbidden fruit. They were afraid and ashamed of what they had done. And so began their troubles with their feelings. In the span of one generation, anger and envy provoked Adam and Eve's son, Cain, to murder his brother, Abel.

Think about it: there were no bad emotions until sin entered the world, but now pain and heartache permeate every aspect of human existence. We feel sin's corrosive effect in the depths of our souls and observe it in the emotions of people all around us—the hurt and loneliness, the fear and anxiety, the grief and depression. We see it in the apprehensive look of a child whose home is full of strife or the tear-stained face of the woman crying at the corner table in the coffee shop. We observe it in the dejected masses crowding onto the subway, and we hear it in the vacant laughter of the lonely trying to hide their pain. Sin is how emotions got so messed up, for Adam and Eve and the rest of us.

Sin has also disrupted the balance of our faculties. The mind, will, and emotions—which were created to work together in complex harmony—now fight against each other. The mind sabotages the emotions with evil thoughts, and the will bullies them both. A bad feeling is powerful enough to overwhelm a rational argument or firm resolve. "Sin plays equal havoc in our understanding, our choosing, and our feeling. It is not that one of them has 'fallen further' than the other two," explains author Os Guinness.[4] Sin also pits the emotions against the body and the body against the emotions. Our sin-cursed bodies can devastate our emotions, and our sin-corrupted emotions can wreck our health (Ps. 38:6–7; Prov. 14:30). Not to mention that Satan exploits every chance he gets to entice us to sin with our emotions.

Emotional pitfalls abound in our sin-pocked world. If we make a bad decision or do something wrong or sinful, we often blame it on our feelings—when actually it is the other way around. We say, "I let my emotions get the better of me," when really, we let sin get the better of our emotions. Emotions are not the source of our problems, but they do have a sin problem. According to theologian John Frame, "My problem is not [my emotions] within me; it is me."[5] The trouble with emotions isn't original. It's original sin. The myth that "emotions are bad" puts the blame in the wrong place. Emotions aren't inherently bad or unruly, but sin has devastated our emotions.

The Stifler and the Junkie

We all have different strategies for trying to deal with our sin-marred emotions. Many of us attempt to stifle our emotions. We don't know how to handle our feelings or express them appropriately, so we shove them into a corner of our lives. Maybe you grew up in a family where nobody showed emotion, or maybe you were made fun of for crying in front of others. Maybe you worry that emotion will hinder your career advancement or hurt your carefully cultivated image of control. Whatever the reason, suppressing your emotions may seem like the best way to handle them. "You almost get the feeling," writes author Matthew Elliot, "that emotions should be kept in cages, like lions at the zoo—nice to walk past and look at, but better left locked up."[6] So lock 'em up is what we do. In fact, we're so proud of stifling our emotions that we boast about it on our T-shirts: Keep Calm and Carry On. Chill. Relax. Stay cool. These are our mottos and our mantras.

But stifling our emotions is hazardous to our spiritual health. A. W. Tozer warned of the consequences: "Be sure that human feelings can never be completely stifled. If they are forbidden their normal course, like a river they will cut another channel through the life and flow out to curse and ruin and destroy."[7] Suppressed feelings do not disappear; they cut new channels and flow out to wreak havoc in our lives. We all know the mess a burst emotional pipe can make. Ulcers and migraines. Family feuds and broken friendships. Anger and retaliation. Theologian D. G. Benner writes, "Emotional suppression is not only the cause of many psychological problems, it should probably also be seen as a sinful response to emotion in that it violates God's intentions."[8] Emotions are not bad; suppressing our emotions is bad. Stifling our emotions is like marking "return to sender" on God's good gift.

While some of us stifle our emotions, others of us put our

feelings on center stage. We take pride in our open, expressive personalities, and we don't hesitate to display our feelings for all the world to see. Maybe we live for the adrenaline rush of euphoric feelings, bouncing from cause to cause, conference to conference, relationship to relationship, in search of the next feel-good experience. We're the "emotion junkies" Bruce and Jodi Ware describe, who are "ruled by the sway of emotional pleasure and pain."[9] For if we get high on good emotions, we just as easily plunge into the depths of despair when things go wrong. In short, what matters most in every decision, relationship, or situation is *how we feel about it.* Our emotions are what we live for and the filter through which we process every moment of our lives.

But God does not want us to live *for* feelings anymore than he wants us to live *without* them. He didn't create our emotions to be paramount, but neither should they languish on the sidelines of our humanity. God gave us emotions as a good gift to be appreciated and employed in balance with our other faculties.

Coming Down from the High and Up from the Low

Exalting our emotions or suppressing them can both be symptoms of a lack of balance in the Christian life. Our faculties are "interdependent," writes Frame. "Each affects the others, and none can function properly apart from the others. When we try to employ one without the others, the result is distorted understanding, choices, and feelings."[10] So if we make reason all-important and the emotions irrelevant, or if we exalt feelings and disdain logic, we are out of balance. In fact, Martyn Lloyd-Jones went so far as to claim that "lack of balance is one of the most fruitful causes of trouble and discord and disquietude in the life of the Christian."[11]

We see a picture of a lack of balance in the two heroines of Jane Austen's *Sense and Sensibility*, Elinor and Marianne. They certainly observed it in each other. Marianne reacted incredulously when Elinor tried to explain her feelings for Edward:

> "I do not attempt to deny," said [Elinor], "that I think very highly of him—that I greatly esteem, that I like him."
>
> Marianne here burst forth with indignation—
>
> "Esteem him! Like him! Cold-hearted Elinor! Oh! Worse than cold-hearted! Ashamed of being otherwise. Use those words again, and I will leave the room this moment."[12]

Later in the story, after Marianne had been deserted by Mr. Willoughby, Elinor tried to exhort Marianne to take control of her emotions:

> "I only wish," replied [Elinor], "there were any thing I *could* do, which might be of comfort to you."
>
> This, as every thing else would have been, was too much for Marianne, who could only exclaim, in the anguish of her heart, "Oh! Elinor, I am miserable indeed," before her voice was entirely lost in sobs.
>
> Elinor could no longer witness this torrent of unresisted grief in silence.
>
> "Exert yourself, dear Marianne," she cried, "if you would not kill yourself and all who love you. Think of your

mother; think of her misery while *you* suffer: for her sake you must exert yourself."

"I cannot, I cannot," cried Marianne; "leave me, leave me, if I distress you; leave me, hate me, forget me! But do not torture me so."[13]

While the sisters each detected the faults in the other, it took them longer to see their own emotional imbalance. So it is with us. We may observe a lack of balance in other people's emotions but fail to perceive it in ourselves. Detecting our own emotional imbalance is more important than we may realize, however, as it is often the key to correcting many of our emotional errors. Maybe we don't see ourselves as the emotion stifler or the emotion junkie; we're not as repressed as Elinor or as hysterical as Marianne. But we all incline toward one extreme or the other. We're all prone to lack emotional balance.

The Gospel Restores My Emotions

Emotions have been disrupted by sin, and so we stifle our feelings or seek emotional highs. But sin does not have the final say. The good news is: through the life, death, and resurrection of Jesus Christ, God erases the guilt of our rebellious emotions, empowers us to resist the temptation to sinful emotions, and enables us to express godly emotions (2 Cor. 5:17). By his grace, we can now receive strength and wisdom to deal with our messed-up feelings, and Christ has promised to one day give us glorified bodies that function perfectly with our emotions (Phil. 3:21).

Jesus didn't save us piecemeal or *a la carte*. He did not

redeem our minds and wills only to leave our emotions to rot on the vine of our humanity. All of our faculties were equally corrupted by sin, but all of them are being equally restored, and Christ makes peace between our minds, wills, and emotions.

Lloyd-Jones exclaimed:

> What a gospel! What a glorious message! It can satisfy man's mind completely, it can move his heart entirely, and it can lead to wholehearted obedience in the realm of the will. That is the gospel. Christ has died that we might be complete men, not merely that parts of us may be saved; not that we might be lop-sided Christians, but that there may be a balanced finality about us.[14]

We need not resign ourselves to stifling or exalting our emotions. Instead, because Christ restores our emotions, they can work the way God always intended, in harmony with our other faculties. To become emotionally balanced we must guard against these two main errors. On the one hand, we must not despise God's good gift of emotions by stifling how we feel; we should receive his gift, make use of it, enjoy it, and explore all that he intends for it to get done in our lives. On the other hand, we must not favor or exalt our emotions. We must not live only to feel, but we should appreciate and apply our minds and wills in equal measure. As Benner writes, "Life gains an intensity and richness" when the emotions function in harmony with the other faculties.[15]

And so we can see that feelings are a good gift from God. But what good is a gift if you don't know how it works? God didn't give us emotions and say, "Have fun figuring them out on your own!" In his Word, he teaches us the marvelous function and purpose for our emotions. Feelings touch every part of us: our knowing and loving and obeying God, our relationships, our work, our play, and our thoughts and decisions. "Emotions are not a luxury. They play a role. . . . Their influence is immense."[16] In the next chapter, we will consider the enormous influence of our emotions on every aspect of life.

3

Why Do I Feel This Way?

A few years ago, Carolyn offered to teach one of her grand-daughters—Janelle's middle daughter, MJ—how to read. Janelle was homeschooling her oldest at the time, and caring for a toddler and baby besides. So every morning MJ went to Mom-Mom's house for kindergarten. At first, MJ could only identify her letters, but she didn't know their sounds or how they fit together. Carolyn and MJ sang phonics songs, made crafts, drilled flash cards, and for the grand finale, went to the zoo for the letter Z. By the end of the school year, MJ was able to read several short stories aloud at one of our weekly family nights. It was a triumph.

Learning how our emotions work is like learning how to read. Our emotions may feel confusing and overwhelming at first, like a page full of words to a beginning reader. We don't know what they mean or what we're supposed to do with them. But when we learn God's purpose for our emotions, a whole new world opens up to us. We can begin to interpret our feelings and discover how they are meant to work with the other faculties. Learning to "read" our emotions will affect every area of our Christian lives and propel us forward in spiritual maturity. So let's go to "feelings school." Let's sharpen our emotional intelligence. Our lesson for today: emotions tell and move.

Emotions Tell Me Who I Am

Emotions are the reporters for the soul. They tell us about ourselves and our world and how we are processing the events in our lives. Before we even form a conscious thought, our emotions are usually on the scene, giving us live updates. They reveal what is going on around us, and shine a light down into the depths of our souls. Emotions tell us who we really are. In other words, our emotions tell us what we value and believe.

First, emotions *tell us what we value.* They tell us about the people we care about and the things in life that we desire. They reveal what we treasure (Matt. 6:21). "Emotion . . . has an object," explains Matthew Elliott, and the strength of the emotion is in proportion to the value of the object.[1]

For example, if we see a small child stray into the street, we feel much stronger emotion than if we see a squirrel run out into the road. We value the child infinitely more than we value the squirrel, and our emotions reflect this reality. They tell us, loud and clear, what we value. Think about it: If your favorite team wins a game, you are excited, but if two teams you don't care about play in the championship, you don't feel much either way. Your team is the object of your emotion. If your child wins an award at school, you feel proud and happy. That's because you value your child. You may feel upset if someone drops one of your fancy dinner plates, but if the same person drops a paper plate, you experience no emotion.

Emotions arise when something happens to the objects we value. In this way, they reveal and report, they *tell* us what we value. Even if we don't know who or what is the object of our emotions, we can be sure there is one. Value determines emotion.

Emotions also *tell us what we believe.* They reveal our take on reality. They tell us how we evaluate what is going on with the people and things that we value. Let's say your mother is late for lunch and isn't replying to your texts. If you interpret these facts to mean that she has been in an accident, you will experience feelings of fear and panic. But if you believe that she is stuck in traffic and her cell phone probably died, you will remain calm. Your feelings rise and fall based on what you believe about a situation. If you think that someone at church doesn't say hi because she is deliberately ignoring you, your feelings may take a dive. But if you happen to know that she has a migraine that morning, you will feel sympathy instead.

Our interpretations make all the difference in our emotions. If we have confidence in the success of a new venture, we will have happy emotions, but if we are doubtful of a good outcome, we will feel glum. If we believe that we aced a test, we will experience relief, but if we are sure that we failed, we will be discouraged. Our emotions emerge from our evaluations of the past, the present, and the future. Emotions talk to us. They tell us what we think. They tell us what we believe.

So this is how it works: our beliefs and values come together to produce our emotions. In other words, *emotions tell us what we think about what we care about*. What we believe about what we value triggers our emotions. The strength of our beliefs together with how much we value the object combine to produce an infinite variety of emotions, weak and strong. Emotions tell us what we value and believe, and how much.

Emotions Tell Me True

Emotions tell, and they tell us the truth. Feelings don't lie, but they may tell us that we believe a lie. Feelings don't confer value, but they tell us that we assess an object as having value. As such, feelings *are* reliable. They accurately tell us about our beliefs and values.

Emotions tell us what is going on inside us. They tell us the truth about who we really are. So emotions that seem unreasonable or irrational are in fact true expressions of an irrational belief or an unreasonable value. We may feel like our emotions are making us crazy, but the real culprits are the beliefs and values from which the emotions spring. According to philosopher Robert Solomon, "Emotions are not irrational; people are irrational."[2]

If emotions tell us who we really are, they also tell us who we are *not*. If the presence of an emotion reveals our beliefs and values, a lack of emotion reveals that we don't really value something or believe that it is true. You can fake it, but you can't manufacture emotion where no belief or value exists. Elliott writes, "If the emotion is missing we can make a legitimate assumption that the claimed value is not really present."[3] For instance, if we say we believe in the importance of Christian fellowship, but we do not desire to hang out with people from church, then we don't value fellowship like we say we do.

Because emotions reveal our beliefs and values (or our lack thereof), they give us vital insight into our hearts. Most important of all, they tell us how we are doing with God. They tell us if we *really* believe God's Word is true, and if we *really* value what God values. Emotions are not the final source of truth, but they do *tell the truth* about us.

Understanding what our emotions are telling us clears up a lot of confusion. Seldom do we have to wonder why we feel the way we do. Instead of asking ourselves, Where did this emotion come from? and getting no answer, we can ask, What does this emotion tell me that I believe and value? and then trace the emotion back to its source. This leads us to *biblical* emotional intelligence. When we locate the beliefs and values that fuel our emotions, we can examine them in light of Scripture and consider whether or not they are pleasing to God.

Emotions Tell Me about My World

Emotions not only tell us about ourselves, but they also tell us about other people and the world around us. Our feelings can help us navigate relationships, make decisions, and even discern problems. For example, let's say we feel unsettled after a conversation with a friend, and, upon reflection, we remember making a comment that may have been misunderstood. So we take action to clear the air. Or a mother may have a nagging feeling that something is wrong with her child, even before she knows all the facts. Her emotions prompt her to question her child, revealing a fear her child was hesitant to share. In both cases, emotions alert the mind which in turn guides the will. "A woman uses her intelligence to find reasons to support her intuition," someone once quipped, and he wasn't far off the mark.[4] While a woman's intuition is not infallible, it should not be ignored. God created us with emotions that are finely tuned to detect problems and discern wisdom for those we love.

Or in decision making, for example, a sense of peace can corroborate our biblical reasons for choosing a new church home. A measure of joy can help confirm a new responsibility or venture we believe to be the will of God. On the flip side, an uneasy feeling about a "too-good-to-be-true" deal may save us from a costly mistake. When our emotions and our minds work together as God intended, they serve as "a sort of internal system of checks and balances," says John Frame.[5] Sometimes emotions take the lead, alerting us to a problem or concern and moving us to action, and sometimes our logic and reason are confirmed by our emotions. Whatever the decision, our goal is to put all the faculties to work in the quest for biblical wisdom.

At the same time, we shouldn't assume that a strong emotion always equals a right emotion, thus elevating our feelings from a faculty to a virtue. This is the "follow-your-heart" approach: If I feel something, it must be right, so I should follow my feelings. For example, "I feel like he's the one for me, so I should marry him, whether or not he is a Christian." An error of this kind can lead to serious consequences.

Neither should we take other people hostage, tying them up with the supposed rightness of our feelings. This is what John Piper calls "emotional blackmail:"[6] If I feel something, it must be right, so you must agree with my feelings. For example, "I feel like you did that because you don't like me, so you must admit that you're wrong." None of us wants to be the object of emotional blackmail, which should deter us from imposing our feelings on others.

Emotions are not the final authority on what is true or worthy of value. Rather, they tell us what *we* think is true, what *we* value. Our emotions don't necessarily tell us the facts about the situation; rather they tell us our interpretations of the facts. Likewise, our emotions don't always tell us what the right values are, but they tell us how much *we* are concerned about certain things. Feelings are true indicators of *our* beliefs and *our* values, not always what is ultimately true or valuable. We should never force other people to bend to the "truth" of our emotions, but rather we must submit our beliefs and values to the truth of God's Word.

Emotions talk, and we should listen. This doesn't mean we do everything they tell us to do or force other people to acquiesce to our feelings. But it does mean that we pay attention and evaluate what our emotions are telling us. If we ignore our feelings, we will miss out on valuable intelligence about our souls and the people around us. We will stunt our growth in maturity and relationships. But when we listen to what our feelings are telling us and evaluate them in light of God's Word, we can grow in godliness.

Emotions Move Me Too

Emotions also move us to action. They propel us forward. "Emotions were given in order to energize behavior and were intended by God to be a catalyst for action," writes D. G. Benner.[7] Feelings are like the engine of the soul. Start 'em up, and you go farther and faster than you could on sheer brains or willpower alone. In fact, the word *emotion* comes from the Latin *movere*, which means "to move."

Feelings are "powerful persuaders," writes Os Guinness.[8] Feelings of compassion move us toward the sufferer; they move us to open our arms in embrace, to cry tears of sorrow, and to serve in practical ways. Fear hurries us through a deserted parking lot or keeps us back from trying something new. Righteous anger drives us to defend the child who is being bullied. Human beings are not programmed machines that move in response to a line of code; rather, as author Robert Kellemen says, "God designed our emotions to put us in motion."[9] Their primary purpose is to turn us away from ourselves and toward God and others in love.

Still, many of us buy into the misconception that to be moved by emotions is a bad thing. As Christians, we are fond of telling each other, "Don't be led by your emotions." This is partially true: we should not be led by our emotions into sin. But emotions *are* supposed to move us. God gave us emotions to move us toward himself in love and obedience. Whether it's a positive emotion, such as joy, or a negative emotion, such as fear, all emotions should drive us to God. "Is anyone cheerful?" asks James. "Let him sing praise" (James 5:13). Or we should follow the psalmist's example: "When I am afraid, I put my trust in you" (Ps. 56:3).

In fact, this is why suppressing our emotions has such negative consequences. It denies the reality of how God created emotions to work. Emotions are not to be stifled or stamped out, but rather they are to propel us to God and godliness. Now, emotions in the grip of sin can be a powerful force in the wrong direction, but even feelings of guilt should drive us to God in repentance. "There is nothing you can feel that you cannot take to God," says counselor Alasdair Groves.[10] And so we should remind each other: *do* be led by your emotions . . . back to God.

So, there you have it: *emotions tell and move*. They tell us what we believe and value. We should listen to what they are telling us and evaluate our emotions in light of Scripture. Emotions also move. We should not try to deny their persuading power, but instead allow them to drive us to God.

When My Emotions Don't Make Sense

While it may sound simple to say that emotions tell and move, emotions aren't always so simple. Sometimes it can feel like we get mixed signals from our emotions. It's as if the channel is scrambled or like they are all yelling at once. So why do emotions feel so confusing at times? For starters, our beliefs and values are complex. What we think about what we care about is shaped by a myriad of factors: family backgrounds, cultures, personalities, and life experiences.

For example, you might come from a Christian or a non-

Christian family, a single-parent or an adoptive home, a family where everyone plays an instrument, excels in sports, or loves the great outdoors. Our backgrounds shape our beliefs and values long before we are even aware of their influence. If you grew up in Great Britain, you might have learned the value of "a stiff upper lip," and if you grew up in Italy, you might have been taught the value of food in bringing the family together. Fictional characters Marilla Cuthbert and Anne Shirley illustrate how different personalities result in a variety of beliefs and values. Anne believed that tomorrow is always fresh with no mistakes in it, while Marilla certainly thought it better not to make any mistakes in the first place.[11]

Life experiences also affect our beliefs and values. For instance, Carolyn was bitten by a Chihuahua when she was little, and to this day she dislikes the breed. Nicole loves to read sports columns to her boys because her dad read them aloud when she was growing up. Something as small as a comment by a family member, friend, or even a stranger can define the way you feel about yourself. A single tragedy will mark your emotions for the rest of your life.

Tim Keller illustrates how different factors can come to bear on our emotional responses:

> People of different personalities, genders, and cultures process emotions differently. They also have different internal values and commitments. A father, for example, may love his children deeply but identify personally more with his career. His wife may be quite dedicated to her vocation but identify her worth more closely with how her children are faring. And so,

if there is a career reversal, the husband may be more "over-thrown" and despondent, while if one of their children gets seriously injured, the mother may be more disconsolate than the father. Same trouble, different responses, because there is a different identity structure within the heart.[12]

An untold number of factors influence our beliefs and values. What we think and care about grows and changes through the years, producing a wide variety of emotions. As Groves puts it, "When you wake up, part of what you bring [to the day] is every other day you have lived."[13] No wonder emotions can be confusing sometimes!

Not only are our beliefs and values complex, but the more complicated our circumstances, the more confusing our emotional responses may seem. Take our friend, Jennifer, for example. She recently moved here to Louisville, Kentucky, from the West Coast. She has left a large, close-knit family, an incredible church and friends, the perfect school for her children, and a "forever babysitter" that her girls adore, and moved to a new city and a house in need of renovations. She and her husband have had to search for a new church, find a new school for their kids, learn the way to the nearest grocery store, and adjust to the sights, smells, tastes, and culture of Louisville. She's still looking for a babysitter. And to top it off, this is her first Christmas away from family.

Jennifer's beliefs and values, which have been shaped through the years by both tragedy and blessing, are now interacting with a new and complex set of circumstances, producing intense and often confusing emotions. She found herself crying after church a few weeks ago, and she still doesn't know why. She's having trouble mapping her tumultuous emotions onto what she's always believed to be true. But Jennifer's emotions aren't broken or misfiring. They are simply responding to a hundred and one new experiences all at once. They are telling her—and telling her truthfully—that she is going through a lot of change in her life right now.

We all have times when life takes a sharp turn: you move to a new house, a new city, or get a new job; you get married or have a baby; you contract an illness or get a pay cut. Dramatic changes, whether pleasant or unpleasant, disrupt our emotions. Even a hectic day or a schedule shift can rattle our feelings. That's because we don't feel in a vacuum: our complex beliefs and values interact with our complex circumstances to produce our emotions. This is how God created emotions to work. As we've already learned, emotions respond. They tell us what is going on and how we are processing life. So when a lot is going on, emotions are going to be talking a lot!

Emotions also affect our bodies, which only adds to their complexity. Sadness rolls down our cheeks, surprise takes our breath away, and anger increases our heart rate. We feel nervousness in the pit of our stomach or our muscles tense in anxiety. And our bodies, in turn, affect our emotions. Our exercise, eating habits, and overall health all influence how we feel. Many of us experience emotional fluctuations, mild to extreme, around our monthly menstrual cycles, pregnancies, postpartum, and menopause.

When our bodies are out of sorts—because of fluctuating

hormones or other health issues—we may need to process our emotions differently. "Since heart and body are interdependent," explains Ed Welch, "a disordered body can shape emotions in such a way that they are unpredictable and unrelated to our desires and loves. In other words, sometimes our emotions are speaking about spiritual matters, and sometimes they are not."[14] A disordered body can give shape to distorted emotions. We need to keep this in mind.

Emotions are remarkably complex. We can't figure out in a day what took a lifetime to develop. We can't respond to fifteen emotional alarms at once. We can't always predict the ways in which our bodies might affect our emotions. And we shouldn't try. We shouldn't try to trace every emotional thread or untangle every emotional knot. It'll never work. Not to mention that all our questioning and analyzing and introspection often pull us into a self-focused spiral. Nowhere in Scripture does God require us to examine and catalog every emotion.

A cacophony of emotions tells us one thing above all: we must move to God. There is no feeling or jumble of feelings that we cannot bring to him. In fact, confusing emotions can be marvelous motivators, driving us to the only one who clears up our confusion. When we move to God in our perplexity and acknowledge that we need his help to understand our emotions, he will graciously help us to hear one or two truths above all the noise. We may not be able to trace the source of every emotion, but we *can* know what God wants us to do with every emotion: bring them to him. And this, friends, is the most important lesson of all.

4

Feeling Good

"I'm over here trying to deal with my out-of-control feelings," a friend wrote to us recently. "I'm having one of those special times when out of nowhere you are off-the-charts overreacting in anger to the dumbest things that yesterday didn't faze you. I mean this is *for real*!" Our friend is a godly woman who is known for her steadfast trust in God, but, like all of us, she has those moments when it feels like her emotions have taken over, hijacking her spiritual progress.

So how do we handle our feelings? How do we fix them when they are broken? How do we keep our emotions from taking control of our lives? The answer: we must start with the One who gave us emotions. It's like buttoning up a blouse—if you get the first button wrong, they will all be askew, but if you get the first one right, the rest line up perfectly. If we don't begin with God, our emotions will be confusing and hard to handle. But when we start with the giver of emotions, our feelings will align with truth. We will feel right, and we will learn how to handle our feelings rightly.

As we already know, emotions are a gift *from God*, which means that our emotions are also *for God*. "For from him and through him and to him are all things. To him be glory forever" (Rom. 11:36). In all that they tell us, and in every way that they move us, emotions are to function for God's glory alone. Because emotions are *from God, for the glory of God*, we must consider how he wants us to feel. This is the place that we must start.

But when it comes to emotions, we tend to start with how *we* feel, how we want to feel, or how others expect us to feel—instead of with God. Because sin permeates our emotions, we're inclined to seek emotions for our sakes, rather than for God's sake. Sin ruins God's good gift by turning our emotions in the wrong direction. Instead of directing our affections toward God, sin turns our emotions toward us. We have the strongest feelings about what *we* want, what *we* fear, what *we* treasure, and what *we* despise. We become, as Martin Luther put it, "curved in" on ourselves. "Sin," he wrote, "bends the best gifts of God toward itself."[1] We take this great gift of emotions and twist it around toward ourselves. We seek emotions for our selfish satisfaction.

Nowhere, perhaps, is this more evident than in the way we talk about our feelings. (Hint—we use a lot of personal pronouns.) I hate how this situation makes me feel. I wish I didn't feel this way. I just want to feel better. I want to feel good about myself. I love how I feel when I'm with him. We obsess over how we feel and how we want to feel. We don't often consider how God wants us to feel. We've taken the good gift that was supposed to be for God's glory and made it all about us.

This, incidentally, is why many of our methods for dealing with difficult emotions often disappoint in the long run. If we go to anger management classes so we can get along better with people or book a trip to the Caribbean so we won't feel down in the winter, we'll only find temporary relief, because our end goal is wrong. As much as we may benefit in the short term from lifestyle changes, they will never truly work if we're trying to fix our emotions for selfish reasons. Even our prayers will be rejected when they are selfishly motivated: "You ask and do not receive, because you ask wrongly, to spend it on your passions" (James 4:3).

But when God saves us, he interrupts our ever-inward, ever-selfish, ever-destructive bent toward ourselves. If we have repented and believed, God changes our hearts and renews our desires, so that we want to move toward him with our emotions. He frees us from our sins so that we can seek after the right emotions for the right reasons. Instead of being stuck in a spiral of selfish emotions, we can live and feel for God. "And he died for all, that those who live might no longer live for themselves but for him who for their sake died and was raised" (2 Cor. 5:15). Emotions were created for the glory of God in the first place, and because of his saving work, they can be expressed for his glory again.

The funny thing is, when we seek the right emotions for God's sake instead of pleasant feelings for our sakes, we get the emotions we desire in the end. As Tim Keller puts Matthew 5:6 in his own words:

> "Happy is the one who seeks not happiness but righteousness." Happiness is a by-product of wanting something more than happiness—to be rightly related to God and our neighbor. If you seek God as the nonnegotiable good of your life, you will get happiness thrown in. If, however, you aim mainly at personal happiness, you will get neither.[2]

Personal fulfillment gets us nowhere, but when we start with God, we can make real progress. When we seek emotions for God and not for ourselves, we will, by the grace of God, find true happiness. Only when we start with God can we handle our emotions; and in his Word, God tells us how we are supposed to feel.

Scripture's Feeling Commands

In a sincere effort to honor God, many of us have assumed that it doesn't matter how we feel, we just need to obey. We've conceived of Christian duty mostly in terms of thoughts, words, and actions, but not feelings. We have unwittingly bought into a common misconception that God doesn't care how we feel—he cares only about what we do in spite of what we feel. But we cannot please God, fulfill the great commandments, or grow in Christlikeness without emotions. Our feelings are essential to obeying God.

Throughout the Bible, God tells us to obey with our emotions. Looking for emotional commands in Scripture is a bit like an egg hunt for toddlers where the eggs are all low to the ground and plainly visible. Once you start looking, you see them everywhere. Here's a sampling of Scripture's commands to feel:

"Hate evil" (Ps. 97:10).
"Serve the LORD with gladness" (Ps. 100:2).
"Mourn with those who mourn" (Rom. 12:15 NIV).
"Be . . . tenderhearted" (Eph. 4:32).
"Let the peace of Christ rule in your hearts" (Col. 3:15).
"Therefore, let us be grateful" (Heb. 12:28).
"Conduct yourselves with fear" (1 Pet. 1:17).

Even though Scripture's landscape is colored with "feeling commands," we tend to think of our emotions as an obedience no-fly zone, as if they don't reside in obedience territory. When we spot a command like, "love your neighbor" (Matt. 22:39) or "rejoice always" (1 Thess. 5:16), we assume that God couldn't possibly be telling us that we're supposed to *feel* loving or joyful. He must mean that we're supposed to put on a happy face and serve others. But these commands pulse with feeling. We are to be tender*hearted*, not merely to show tenderness. We are to have *feelings* of peace that rule our hearts, not simply have a calm demeanor. We are to have strong *emotions* against evil and sin, not only refrain from sinful actions. The apostle Paul commended the Christians in Rome not only for their acts of obedience but also for their godly emotions: "[you] have become obedient from the heart" (Rom. 6:17).

John Piper uses 1 Corinthians 13, the famous passage on love, to make this point:

The very definition of love in 1 Corinthians refutes this narrow conception of love. For example, Paul says love is not *jealous* and not easily *provoked* and that it *rejoices* in the truth and *hopes* all things (13:4–7). All these are *feelings*! If you feel things like unholy jealousy and irritation, you are not loving. And if you do not feel things like joy in the truth and hope, you are not loving. In other words, *yes*, love is more than feelings; but, *no*, love is not less than feelings.[3]

We cannot be content with half-truths about our emotions. Obedience is more than feelings, but obedience is not less than feelings. God doesn't command our minds and our wills and then give us a free pass when it comes to our emotions. He calls us to obedience with every one of our faculties, including our emotions. If our feelings are from God and for God, then we must feel—and not just think and act—the way he tells us to feel.

Scripture's feeling commands raise the godliness bar considerably. So high, it's scary. We may have thought we were within striking distance of many of the *actions* required by Scripture. After all, we "show hospitality" (Rom. 12:13); we are "not neglecting to meet together" (Heb. 10:25); we do "good works" (1 Tim. 6:18); and we "let no corrupting talk come out of [our] mouths" (Eph. 4:29). We all admit we've got our fair share of weaknesses and sins, but we think, on average, we are pretty good Christians. When we include Scripture's feeling commands in our evaluations, however, the results change.

No matter how much we serve or sacrifice, if we don't *feel* the emotions God wants us to feel, our acts of service fall short of the obedience he requires. The Israelites' *lack of feeling* actually provoked God's righteous condemnation: "Because you did not serve the LORD your God with joyfulness and gladness of heart . . . therefore you shall serve your enemies . . . lacking everything" (Deut. 28:47–48). Yikes! God never intended for us to perform our duties grudgingly, without feeling or emotion. He did not create us with the faculty of emotion only to have us leave it out of the Christian life. Rather, God designed our feelings to play a central role in our service to him.

When Good Feelings Are Bad . . . and Vice Versa

So what do godly emotions feel like? For starters, we know that God wants us to have positive emotions such as love, joy, and peace, right? Yes, but did you also realize there are positive emotions we are *not* supposed to feel? We tend to think a Christian is someone who feels "up" and "happy" all the time, but Scripture tells us there are times when we should *not* be happy—for example, "Do not rejoice when your enemy falls" (Prov. 24:17). And there are also things for which we should *not* feel love such as, "love no false oath" (Zech. 8:17).

In the same way, we may imagine that God disapproves of negative feelings such as hate, anger, and jealousy. That's true, sometimes. But it may surprise you that other times God *commands* us to feel negative emotions such as anger and hate. We are to "be angry" (Eph. 4:26) and to "abhor what is evil" (Rom. 12:9). In short, "there is . . . a time to love, and a time to hate" (Eccles. 3:1, 8). Contrary to what we may have believed,

Christians should be lovers *and* haters. Clearly, God doesn't evaluate our emotions like we do.

So if happy emotions aren't always right, and unhappy emotions aren't always wrong, then how do we know if we feel godly or not? It's quite simple really: *godly emotions arise from godly beliefs and values.* In other words, godly emotions spring from beliefs and values that correspond to the truths and values of God's Word. By the same token, ungodly emotions flow from ungodly beliefs and values. The money question is this: Do we believe what God says is true and do we value what God says we should value? If so, we will have *true feelings*.

In other words, our positive emotions are ungodly if we approve of things that God says are wrong or find pleasure in things that God hates. If we are happy at the downfall of someone we dislike, if we delight in a juicy bit of gossip, or if we find enjoyment in a TV show's depiction of sinful behavior, then our positive emotions are not set on godly beliefs and values. Here is where our emotions often reveal who we truly are: What makes us happy? What do we love? What pleases us? What do we get excited about? If our positive emotions are centered around ungodly values, or if our hopes are set on ungodly beliefs, then these feelings are not pleasing to God.

On the flip side, our negative emotions are godly when they rise up in opposition to sin and suffering. So it is right to grieve over the tragedy of abortion and the injustice of racism. We should be angry at pornography and sex trafficking. We should be disgusted by slander and gossip. We should feel heartsick whenever God's truth and biblical values are rejected or violated. In fact, to lack negative emotions in any of these cases would reveal a lack of moral character on our part. "It would be impossible . . . for a moral being to stand in the presence of perceived wrong indifferent and unmoved," wrote theologian B. B. Warfield.[4] How often, to our shame, do we all lack the negative emotions that God requires? Pastor Clifford Pond wrote, "It is at the level of our emotions that our imperfections are most clearly exposed. We are pained at the wrong things, we laugh at the things that should make us angry. This is a true barometer of our purity of mind and too often it finds us wanting."[5]

So our anger may be godly or ungodly; our feelings of love and affection may be godly or ungodly; our sadness may be right (more on this in chap. 8), and our happiness may be wrong; even our jealousy and our anxiety may be godly depending on the beliefs and values behind them (Song 8:6; 1 Cor. 7:34). How can we tell if we have the right emotions? Not by whether we "feel good." We must ask, What do I believe that is making me happy or sad? and, What do I value that is causing these emotions? When we learn to evaluate our emotions—not by whether they are positive or negative, but by how they reflect our beliefs and values—it will be easy for us to see the emotions that God requires.

Not only should we have the right kinds of feelings, but we should also feel with the right intensity. All of our emotions "ought to be proportioned to the real value of their objects," explains professor Mark Talbot.[6] "For example, virtually everyone recognizes that there is something really wrong with spouses who don't love their husbands or wives much more than they love their dogs or with parents who aren't much more emotionally involved with their children than with their cars."[7] In other words, we should feel most strongly about the most important things. So let's ask ourselves, What do I feel most strongly about? or, more importantly, *Who* do I feel most strongly about? Scripture tells us what the answer should be: "You shall love the Lord your God with all your heart and with all your soul and with all your strength and with all your mind, and your neighbor as yourself" (Luke 10:27). When we feel what God wants us to feel, as strongly as he wants us to feel it, we will have godly emotions.

Feeling What God Wants Me to Feel

Of course, every Christian *wants* to obey with her emotions, but *how* do we feel what God wants us to feel? Can we really change how we feel? We think of emotion as something that simply happens, not something we can make happen. Feelings come, and feelings go, and we are just hanging on for the ride. We can't say "be happy" and then feel happy emotions. We can't produce sympathy or godly anger on demand. We can't tell our feelings to respond in the same way that we tell our minds to focus or our feet to move. Feelings don't work like that. Everyone knows you can't eliminate sad feelings or generate happy feelings on demand.

While it's true that we can't change our emotions directly, we *can* change the beliefs and values that fuel our emotions. This is how we obey with our feelings. When we understand that emotions arise from beliefs and values, we can go after our emotions at their source. We can target the beliefs and values that lead to ungodly feelings. We can cultivate beliefs and values that lead to godly feelings. Change our beliefs and values, and we change our emotions.

Because we can change our beliefs and values, we are morally responsible for our emotions. For example, if we choose to believe a slanderous report we read on the Internet and experience feelings of outrage over wrongs that may never have been committed, we are morally responsible for those emotions; they are based on false testimony, which Scripture forbids us to entertain. Similarly, if we feel delighted at someone else's misfortune, we are responsible for those emotions; they are based on a sinful value from which we can and should repent. We are accountable to God for how we feel.

Just as a rudder directs the course of a massive ship, so too our beliefs and values form the rudder that changes our emotional direction. Some beliefs and values are more easily dislodged, and our emotions change quickly. Other beliefs and values are deeply entrenched in our souls, influenced by years of reinforcement. But there is no belief or value that can ultimately resist God's grace. By the power of the Holy Spirit, our emotions can "be transformed by the renewal of [our minds]" (Rom. 12:2). When we believe what God commands us to believe and value what God commands us to value, we will have godly emotions.

Scripture's commands to feel are not one more thing to add to our Christian to-do lists or one more way to make us feel condemned; rather, they are encouraging and exciting. Who of us doesn't want to have the love for Christ and compassion for others that God commands? These godly emotions are not a special talent handed out to a group of elite Christians. While none of us can muster up a talent that we don't possess, we can all have godly emotions. That's because emotions are not a talent; they are a faculty. And, as you'll remember, God has given us the faculty of emotions as a gift, and he has redeemed our emotions for his glory. Piper says, "Conversion is the creation of new desires, not just new duties; new delights, not just new deeds; new treasures, not just new tasks."[8]

What's more, God doesn't give us a command and then leave us to try to fulfill it on our own. As Augustine put it, God gives what he demands.[9] If God demands that we feel godly emotions, that means he intends to give us godly emotions. By the power of the Holy Spirit, we can cultivate godly feelings and mortify ungodly feelings. We *can* feel the way God wants us to feel. The apostle Paul exclaims, "His divine power has granted to us all things that pertain to life and godliness" (2 Pet. 1:3). "All things" includes godly emotions. We have been granted the power to obey with our feelings. Just as we can think godly thoughts and make godly choices, we can feel godly emotions. How we do that—how we actually change our emotions—is the focus of our remaining chapters.

5

Emotional Emergency Measures

It was the semifinal game of the Commonwealth Cup soccer tournament. Nicole's son, Jack, and Kristin's son, Owen, were playing for the Sawyer Strikers—a team coached by their uncle, Chad. The two of us were standing on the sidelines at midfield, yelling boisterous encouragement to each player in turn. We're not what you'd call *quiet* fans, so it wasn't until halftime when we noticed that the parents sitting in front of us were not amused by our enthusiastic cheering. They turned to us and snapped: "Are you going to be yelling for the rest of the game? If so, we're moving." Taken aback, we both felt embarrassed at first, and then angry. We sarcastically replied: "We're *so sorry*." With that, the couple huffily packed up their chairs and marched away. We did feel sorry, later. If only we hadn't been sarcastic. If only we had demonstrated the love of Christ.

We all have moments like this. We're enjoying life, and then someone comes along who provokes us. We're suddenly awash in a rip current of frustrating emotions. We don't know what our feelings are telling us, but we do know they are moving us in the wrong direction. We just don't know what to do about it. Os Guinness describes it this way: "The emotions rise up against reason in their own special kind of 'palace coup' within the personality. Then they carry everything before them in a flood of feeling that overwhelms logic and reason." He continues, "Reason is cut down, obedience is thrown out, and for a while the rule of the emotions is as sovereign as it is violent. The coup d'état is complete."[1] We surrender to our sinful emotions and get caught in an even more vicious cycle of discouragement and regret.

Here is where all our good intentions to obey God with our feelings often go wrong. We may raise our voices, make a snarky comment, or withdraw from others. As one woman wrote to us, "All the verses I read and store up in my more rational moments seem to go out the window as soon as I am annoyed or emotional, and worst of all I have no desire to get back in control." That's the worst of it—not only do we forget everything we know when we are in an emotional rip current, we may not even *want* to remember. And we can hardly stop, sit down with our Bibles, and figure out the beliefs and values behind our emotions. But even in temptation, we can still choose emotional obedience. By God's grace, we can turn these moments of potential failure into opportunities to grow in godly emotions.

Watch Out for Emotional Temptation

The warning sign at the beach reads, "Rip currents—Watch Out—You could be swept out to sea and drown. If in doubt, don't go out!" Jesus also told his disciples to watch out for danger: "Watch and pray that you may not enter into temptation. The spirit indeed is willing, but the flesh is weak" (Matt. 26:41). Emotional temptation isn't strange or unusual; Scripture tells us to expect it. Even though we have a new spirit within us that wants to obey, our flesh is still weak. So we should not be surprised by temptation, but rather we should *watch for it*.

For starters, we should avoid or eliminate predictable sources of emotional temptation. As the sign says, "If in doubt, don't go out!" Or as Scripture puts it, "flee" temptation (1 Cor. 6:18). So if we frequently get impatient with our children when rushing them out the door to school, then maybe we should change our morning routines. If our daily intake of "breaking news" is tempting us to fear, perhaps we should shut it off. Or if our social media habits cause us to feel discontent, then maybe we should stop checking our phones.

But then there are tempting situations we can't avoid, such as dinner with the in-laws, stresses at work, caring for the children all day (and all night)—or temptations we don't expect, like a rude comment, an unforeseen bill, or a lost set of keys. For times like these, we need a quick response plan already in place: a plan that is straightforward and clear and helps us triage the problem. We might call such a plan our "emergency measures." Emergency measures can protect us from sin and regret (even when confronted with angry soccer parents!), and position us to change our emotions.

"No temptation has overtaken you that is not common to man. God is faithful, and he will not let you be tempted beyond your ability, but with the temptation he will also provide the way of escape, that you may be able to endure it" (1 Cor. 10:13). *No* temptation—and that includes emotional temptation—has overtaken us that is not common to every other Christian. And God will not let us be tempted beyond our ability. No matter how strong the emotion, we *can* overcome temptation by taking the way of escape that God provides. Here are three practical emergency measures for resisting emotional temptation.

1. CHOOSE SELF-CONTROL

The first emergency measure is to exercise self-control. It means we employ what Elisabeth Elliot called "the swift, hard renunciation—*I will not.*"[2] No matter how strong the emotion, no matter how overwhelming the situation, we can choose not to sin. Self-control will stop the emotional rip current from pulling us out into a sea of consequences, but if we fail to exercise self-control, we may place ourselves in even greater danger. Using a land-bound image, Proverbs warns us that without self-control we are "like a city broken into and left without walls" (Prov. 25:28).

Self-control resists the first rise of a sinful emotion. It means we take no sinful action: no revenge or retaliation, no abrupt decisions or reckless behavior, no impulsive emails or rash tweets. And we refuse to sin with our mouths. We don't vent or complain or lash out—no matter how "good" it might feel in the moment. We don't gossip about the person who hurt us. We hold back the comeback. If necessary, we don't even speak.

When Janelle's oldest daughter, Caly, was a toddler, she had frequent outbursts of anger. In an attempt to help her overcome her emotional temptation, Janelle taught Caly one simple habit: as soon as Caly's emotions began to escalate, Janelle would tell her to "cover her mouth." After lots of training, Caly learned to clap her hand over her mouth, and almost immediately she would begin to calm down. Once she got control of her emotions, Caly could listen to her mom address the source of her anger. Today, Caly has become much more self-controlled in the face of temptation (more mature than her grandmother and aunt, sometimes!). We, too, can learn to *choose self-control* and, in effect, "cover our mouths" at the first risings of sinful emotions.

Self-control is a "fruit of the Spirit" (Gal. 5:22–23) that rarely gets a shout-out these days. Many people respond with disdain to the idea of self-control. They think that expressing whatever we feel, without forethought, is a virtue. "I'm just being real, honest, and authentic," they say. By contrast they often—wrongly—equate self-control with suppression, being fake, or putting up a false front. But exercising self-control doesn't mean we deny that what we feel is real; instead, as philosopher David Pugmire says, we "refuse to identify with the verdict of [our] emotions."[3] Self-control isn't suppression; rather, it's a refusal to agree with the sinful beliefs and values behind our emotions. Self-control says to our sinful emotions: I might not know why I feel this way, but I know one thing, you are sinful. I know you come from a sinful belief and a sinful value and I intend to fight you. This is my first resistance.

By the grace of God, we can choose self-control. It's simple, it's effective, and it's achievable. "Obedience to God is always possible," wrote Elliot. "It is a deadly error to fall into the notion that when feelings are extremely strong we can do nothing but act on them."[4] As Paul told Timothy, "For God gave us a spirit not of fear but of power and love and self-control" (2 Tim. 1:7).

2. CRY OUT TO GOD

When we are in the throes of emotional temptation—when "the rule of the emotions is as sovereign as it is violent"—we need more than a few good tips.[5] The situation is desperate. The temptation is bigger than we can handle on our own. And the potential consequences are serious, for temptation leads to sin, and sin leads to death (James 1:14–15). We need rescue. We need saving. And the good news is, all we have to do is ask. "Save me, O God!" the psalmist prayed. "For the waters have come up to my neck. I sink in deep mire, where there is no foothold; I have come into deep waters, and the flood sweeps over me" (Ps. 69:1–2). As a drowning woman calls for help, we must cry to the Lifeguard of our souls to rescue us from our emotional rip currents. Usually, in an emotional emergency, we only have time to throw up a quick, desperate (often silent) prayer: *"Save me, O God!"* But it's enough. He hears, and he will come to our rescue. As David testified, "He sent from on high, he took me; he drew me out of many waters" (Ps. 18:16).

"Let us learn . . . that prayer is the best practical remedy that we can use in time of trouble," wrote pastor J. C. Ryle.[6] For one, the act of praying itself has an immediate effect on our emotions. It pulls us out of a self-centered spiral and redirects our attention to God. When we pray, we move to God, which is the purpose for our emotions in the first place. And prayer doesn't just move us toward God; it moves God toward us (James 4:8). Prayer calls down the attentive help of our heavenly Father.

Through prayer, God grants us the strength to exercise self-control. He also gives us the grace to respond with kindness to unexpected trouble. When we cry to God for help, we can push back the violent tide of sinful emotions. We can even experience an instantaneous change in how we feel. So if, as James tells us, "The prayer of a righteous person has great power as it is working" (James 5:16), why would we not cry out to God in every emotional temptation?

Not only should we pray in an emergency, we should also pray every day that God would keep us from temptation in the first place. "Watch and pray, that you may not enter into temptation," Jesus urged his disciples (Matt. 26:41). No doubt this is why the Lord's Prayer includes the request, "Lead us not into temptation, but deliver us from evil" (Matt. 6:13). Temptation is serious, but prayer—that God would spare us and deliver us—is the best practical remedy. Let's cry out to our Savior today.

3. TAKE ONE ACTION

After we exercise self-control and cry out to God, our third emergency measure is to take *one* action to diffuse the sinful feeling. We may not have a lot of time to think in an emergency, but we can take one simple step of obedience. Like a pin to a balloon, a single word or action can release the pressure from emotional temptation.

In some cases, we should do the opposite of whatever we feel like doing. So if you feel like criticizing, say something complimentary; if you feel like complaining, say something grateful; if you feel like withdrawing, start a conversation; if you feel like brooding, sing a hymn. To do the opposite of what you feel may feel like the hardest thing to do, but it has an immediate effect. Imagine if the two of us had said a kind word to the angry soccer parents instead of making a sarcastic remark. Not only would we have thrown a damper on our own angry feelings, we would have defused their anger as well. "A soft answer turns away wrath, but a harsh word stirs up anger" (Prov. 15:1). Or let's say you have a conflict with your husband. You may feel like spewing angry, bitter words, but what if you did the opposite and reached out to hold his hand instead? This single, affectionate gesture would break the back of your frustration and most likely soothe his anger as well.

Or, as an old Saxon poem puts it, we may need to "do the next thing." Get out of bed. Wash the dishes. Start a load of laundry. Take the dog for a stroll. Walk away from the conflict. In other words, take one action to turn from temptation and toward something constructive. This may strike you as an unspiritual suggestion, but it is straight out of the Bible: "Turn away from evil and do good" (Ps. 34:14). In other words, do whatever good, useful, productive, mundane thing you are supposed to be doing right now instead of giving in to emotions of anger, self-pity, fear, or depression. Our hearts may be racing with envy, or our heads may be clouded in despair, but as we turn away from emotional temptation and toward one right action, the strength of our sinful feelings will begin to dissipate.

When the trials of life collide with our beliefs and values to produce temptation, emergency measures can help us fight back. They are the first line of defense against sinful emotions. Instead of getting stuck in a cycle of sin and regret, we can choose to exercise self-control, cry out to God, and take one action. Once we are out of immediate danger, we can prayerfully consider why we were tempted and how we can change our beliefs and values for the future.

Think about a recurring temptation you face in the midst of your emotional rip currents. Maybe you are tempted to be irritable or get angry, shrink back in fear, or cave to anxiety. We can prepare ahead to meet these temptations with emergency measures. When do you need to have emergency measures at the ready? What is one situation in which you can begin to exercise self-control, cry out to God, and take one action? If we put emergency measures to work in the moment of emotional temptation, we will be surprised by the difference that they can make. No longer do we need to repeat the same sins over and over again. We can chart a new course and begin to change our emotions.

Case Study: From Menstruation to Menopause

If ever there is a time for emergency measures, it's during those times in our lives when we deal with fluctuating hormones. Many of us know what it feels like to live with two versions of ourselves. Our friend Katie's husband labeled the two versions of his wife "Katie A" and "Katie B." While Katie A was the everyday version, the hormonal Katie B showed up once a month. Katie A was easygoing, quick-witted, and quick-to-laugh. Katie B was quick-to-cry, irritable, and stressed. If emotions "tell," then Katie A and Katie B told very different stories.

Hormonal fluctuations like Katie's can cause physical pain and weakness, as well as emotional challenges. For some women, the suffering is severe. Maybe PMS claims two weeks out of the month to wreak havoc on your body and emotions. Or maybe you experience the exhilaration of bringing life into the world, only to fall into a hormonally induced depression. Some women have their emotions turned upside down by menopause.

Every hormonal trial is also a temptation, and a big temptation at that. It's a time when sin seeks to exploit our bodies' weakness. So how do we respond in a godly manner during these difficult times in our lives? While some may benefit from medical attention, we all need biblical wisdom to navigate the emotional extremes that sometime accompany these physical changes. During PMS, we must take responsibility for our emotions, but we must not take our emotions too seriously. When we are hormonal, our disordered bodies are often shaping our emotions.[7] We aren't crazy or out of control or a different person; our emotions are simply telling us that we're under the intense pressure of a physical trial. To chart a straight course through hormonal waters, we may want to think about avoiding the shoals of *outbursts* on the one side and the rocks of *introspection* on the other.

When we're hormonal, we may often be more tempted to sinful outbursts. We might lash out in anger or react irritably at the slightest provocation. In a surge of despair or self-pity, we may say things we know to be false about God, other people, or ourselves. Or we may panic, succumbing to outsized feelings of fear. Even if our hormonal emotions may not be speaking to spiritual matters, our responses still matter to God.[8] We are not free to express these feelings in a sinful manner, no matter how strong.

The temptation to sin may seem irresistible during menstruation or menopause, but God's grace is sufficient to help us overcome. "Bodily problems are not powerful enough to make us sin or keep us from living by faith," writes Ed Welch.[9] Remember the comforting words of 1 Corinthians 10:13: hormonal temptations are common, but God is faithful. He will provide a way of escape, and he will help us to endure. When we realize that we are prone to overreact during these times, we can exercise self-control, cry out to God, and take one action. In this way, we can protect our souls and our relationships from the consequences of sinful eruptions.

We also need to resist the tendency toward introspection. In the next chapter, we will consider how to evaluate our sinful emotions, but hormonal times are *not* good times to assess our spiritual progress. If we try to take our spiritual pulses when we are hormonal, we'll probably get an inaccurate reading. Our emotions may tell us that we've fallen back into old habits, that we are failures, or that we aren't even Christians. But emotions don't speak accurately about spiritual matters when they are affected by a disordered body. PMS is not the time to figure out why we feel the way we do or to go dumpster diving in the depths of our souls.

Hormonal emotions are also notorious for sending bad signals about the people in our lives. We may come to faulty conclusions about what our friends mean by their comments or what our husbands intend by their actions (or inaction). But people aren't usually as insensitive or unloving as they may appear when we're hormonal. Neither has God backed off for a while; rather, our physical states may have diminished our ability to sense his presence. "What we should be clear about," insists John Piper, "is that the condition of our bodies makes a difference in the capacity of our minds to think clearly and of our souls to see the beauty of hope-giving truth."[10] We must not underestimate the impact that the body can have on our emotions. Thankfully, God does not distance himself from us in these times. In our weakness, he will sustain us.

The bottom line is this: we can honor God, even when we are hormonal. With his help we can resist the temptation to sinful outbursts and fruitless introspection and wait quietly until the emotional storm has blown over. Things will look a lot different in the morning.

How Do I Control My Emotions?

Meet Charity. She's struggling with her emotions.

I have the most trouble controlling my emotions with my mother. I am thirty, have been married for five years, and have a baby on the way, but since high school I have had difficulty in my relationship with my mother. Over the years this has often resulted in big blow ups—yelling matches— either in person or over the phone. I've been trying to work on how I respond to my mom over the last five years, but my question is: How am I supposed to control my emotions when my mom cannot control hers and doesn't show any interest in working on the way she responds to me? How do you even begin to deal with the other person without becoming bitter, frustrated, or upset?

What if your mother tries to guilt you all the time and no amount of giving on your part is ever enough? What if the relationship is supposed to be all about pleasing her and obedience to her whims, even when you are married? How can an adult child show honor to an "unreasonable" parent? I feel sometimes like I'm the more mature individual in the relationship.

How do I control my emotions? Charity wants to know. It's not easy to be the mature one when relating to a parent, and we sympathize with Charity's ongoing battle to control her emotions. How should Charity and the rest of us deal with the difficult feelings that swirl around a conflict-riddled relationship or any challenging circumstance for that matter? How do we escape the grip of envy or get off the treadmill of anxiety? How do we cope with a sadness that never seems to lift?

We hope it's clear by now: we *can* change how we feel. We don't have to rely on knee-jerk (and unbiblical) methods of suppressing or venting. We don't have to eat through a box of donuts to get out of a funk or drown our sorrows in a glass of wine and a TV binge. We don't have to splash our emotions all over social media and feel the residue of regret in the morning. We don't have to live as a victim of our emotions. Relying on the power of the Holy Spirit, we can learn to obey with our feelings.

Emergency measures are the first line of defense. We can choose self-control, prayer, and swift action in the heat of the moment to counteract temptation. Then, after the crisis has passed, we can go after the beliefs and values that lurk beneath our sinful emotions and target them for change. When we change our beliefs and values, over time, our emotions will begin to change.

Of course, none of this can happen apart from the grace of God. Only he can help us to see our sinful beliefs and values. Only he can forgive the guilt of our rebellious emotions. Only he can lead us to repentance and infuse us with power to change. But the good news is that he can and he will! The God who gave us the gift of emotions in the first place is eager to give us the grace that renews and restores our emotions.

So let's roll up our sleeves and get to work. The purpose of this chapter is to help us figure out *what* our beliefs and values actually are and *how* they need to change. We'll ask (and hopefully learn how to answer) two simple questions: *What do I really believe and value?* and *Do my beliefs and values line up with God's Word?* These questions aren't a formula that automatically generates new emotions, but they do help us get to the root of what's causing our fears and our flare-ups, our melancholy and our mood swings. When we locate our sinful beliefs and values, look at them in light of Scripture, and turn to God in repentance, we can make real, measurable progress in dealing with our emotions.

What Do I Really Believe and Value?

Most of the questions we ask ourselves each day call for quick answers: What should I make for dinner? Which shoes look better with my blouse? How long will it take me to finish this project? Ask. Answer. Go. But the questions in this chapter are of the pondering kind, meant to be reflected upon at length and revisited from time to time. Picture Winnie the Pooh in his Thotful Spot, tapping his head and muttering, "Think, think, think." So as you read this chapter, don't worry about trying to absorb all of the questions and verses at once; instead, we hope you will regularly return to and benefit from this content.

For starters, choose an emotion you struggle with but that you know is wrong. You want to feel what God wants you to feel, but honestly, you just don't. Perhaps you wake up every day feeling grumpy, or maybe you feel a surge of jealousy every time you see your coworker, or maybe you often feel irritable toward your children.

If we want to get to the source of what we feel, we need to figure out what we believe and value. Let's start by considering our beliefs. To identify the beliefs behind our sinful emotions we can ask: What do I think about this person or situation? What do I believe? Not what we are *supposed* to believe, but what we *really* believe: our raw, unedited thoughts about it all.

For example, we might ask ourselves, What do I *really* believe? and come up with answers such as: God doesn't love me. My circumstances will never change. I just can't take it anymore. I'm a failure. I don't deserve to be treated like this. Things are only going to get worse. I'm never going to feel better.

Sound familiar? We've all had thoughts like these. We may feel uncomfortable admitting them, but in order to pinpoint what is sinful about our beliefs, we first need to be honest about what we actually believe. Only when we drag these beliefs out into the open can we deal with them.

Next, to determine our values, we can ask: What do I *really* want? Our values are anything we prize—a relationship, experience, goal, or possession. They're the fill-in-the-blanks of "All I want is _____." Or "If only _____, then I would be happy." Or "I wish _____."

If we ask, What do I *really* want? our answers may sound something like: All I want is a husband who understands me. I wish my job was more fulfilling. I wish I had a bigger home and a better income. If only I could lose more weight. I wish I got more likes on Instagram. All I want is a little appreciation. If only I had friends.

When we ask, What do I really believe and value? the answers we get aren't always so pretty. But only when we face up to what we truly think and want can we begin to change our feelings. If we try to stab at vague emotions, we won't get far, but when we take a good hard look at our actual beliefs and values in light of Scripture, we can discover where they've gone wrong. As counselor David Powlison says, "Change happens in specifics."[1]

Once we name our beliefs and values, we must take them to Scripture and ask: *Do my beliefs and values line up with God's Word?* Scripture exposes the "thoughts and intentions"—the beliefs and values—of our hearts (Heb. 4:12). As Elisabeth Elliot once said, "The Word of God I think of as a straight edge, which shows up our own crookedness. We can't really tell how crooked our thinking is until we line it up with the straight edge of Scripture."[2] Wherever our thinking and desires fall askew of Scripture's straightedge, there we find our sinful emotions.

Do My Beliefs Line Up with God's Word?

A sinful belief is a lie that sets itself up against God's truth. We must learn to detect the lies we believe so that we can bring them to Scripture and straighten them out.

If we trace back all our sinful emotions to their source, we will find *lies about God*. We may not even realize we harbor lies about God—we are Christians after all, which means we believe in God. The thing is, our *formal* beliefs about God don't always match our *functional* beliefs—our everyday working beliefs—about God. We sing in church that he is all powerful, but then we doubt he can rescue us from our difficult situations. We talk about his love to others, but then we secretly wonder if he really loves us. The wider the space between what we *say* we believe about God and what we *really* believe about God, the more room there is for sinful emotions to fester.

For instance, we may testify of God's love, but after years of infertility, conflict with another person, or financial difficulty, we may start to believe the lie that "God doesn't care." Because if God truly cared, wouldn't he have answered my prayers and fixed this situation by now? A lie like this, if it lodges in our hearts, will spawn emotions of anger, frustration, and even despair.

To extricate ourselves from these feelings, we need to bring our wrong beliefs to God's straightedge: "He cares for you," Scripture says (1 Pet. 5:7). "And we know that for those who love God all things work together for good" (Rom. 8:28). If we truly believe that God cares for us and that he causes all things to work for good, we can stamp out the lie that God doesn't care, and the fog of despair will eventually give way to the sunshine of hope.

Lies about God branch out into other lies—about ourselves and our circumstances—all of which provoke sinful emotions. Some of the hardest lies to detect are *lies about ourselves*. We absorb messages from family members, the media, and our culture without realizing it, and these beliefs shape how we feel about ourselves. Here's a typical lie that women are tempted to believe: "My worth is based on my performance." Do you ever think that your worth is based on how well you perform in school, or as a wife and mother, or in your job? The first sign that we believe this lie is often the shame and dismay we feel when we fail. But it can just as easily be the happiness we find in our successes. Either way, the lie of "performance equals worth" jerks the chain of our emotions.

Only when we set this lie next to Scripture's straightedge can we begin to see its mangled shape. We are to "put no confidence in the flesh" (Phil. 3:3)—not in our performances, or our abilities, or even our obedience. Our best performances will always fall short, pulling our emotions down with them. The only way to true peace and joy is to trust in the performance of another: "not having a righteousness of my own that comes from the law, but that which comes through faith in Christ" (Phil. 3:9).

Many of us believe *lies about our circumstances*. We carry

around underlying assumptions about what makes life mean-ingful, how things should go for us, or how other people should treat us. But often these beliefs do not line up with God's Word. For example, when something bad happens to us, we often say to ourselves: "Life isn't fair." In other words, "I don't deserve what's happening to me right now." Then we repeat this lie the next time things don't go our way. Is it any wonder we feel resentful, discouraged, and hopeless about the future? These emotions don't come out of the blue; they grow and strengthen every time we reinforce this lie about life.

What does Scripture say we deserve? "The wages of sin is death." But what have we received instead? "The free gift of God is eternal life in Christ Jesus our Lord" (Rom. 6:23). As sinners, we deserve death and judgment, but "for our sake he made him to be sin who knew no sin, so that in him we might become the righteousness of God" (2 Cor. 5:21). Talk about unfair! We do not deserve the righteousness of Christ, but that is what we have been given. When we repeat this glorious gospel truth to ourselves each day, our hearts will be filled with wonder and gratitude.

Take some time to write down and consider the following: What are my working beliefs about God? How do I think about myself? What do I think about how things are going for me? How do my beliefs line up with the life-giving truth of the gospel?

The good news is this: when we realign our beliefs with God's Word—throwing out the lies and choosing to believe what God's Word says is true—our emotions will change. In a series of couplets, the psalmist lays out the beauty of truth and its emotional impact: "The law of the LORD is perfect, reviving the soul . . . the precepts of the LORD are right, rejoicing the heart" (Ps. 19:7–8). God's Word is perfect and right, bringing joy and revival to the emotions. What glorious hope! When we bring our crooked, sinful beliefs to God's Word, the Word goes to work on our emotions.

Do My Values Line Up with God's Word?

Once we identify what our values are, we can take them to Scripture and ask, What does God's Word say about these values? We all know that Scripture categorically forbids certain sinful desires such as covetousness, envy, and lust (Gal. 5:17–21; Col. 3:5–9). These evil desires have one thing in common: we want something that doesn't belong to us. So, for example, we are not to covet someone else's laptop, envy someone else's good looks, or lust after someone else's husband. God has not given those things to us; therefore, we are forbidden to want them.

We can recognize a forbidden value easily enough, but we don't always perceive a good value that has turned sinful. That's the tricky thing about many of our sinful values—they might initially look good, right, and even admirable. But the crookedness of our values often becomes apparent when we line them up next to God's Word. Scripture challenges us to consider not only *what* we want but also *who* we want it for (James 4:3). Do we want it to please God or to please ourselves (Rom. 15:1; Gal. 1:10)? Do we want it for God's glory or our own selfish satisfaction (Ps. 119:36; Phil. 2:3)? Remember, as Luther said, that remaining sin inclines us to selfishness; it "bends the best gifts of God toward itself."[3] So a sinful value is any object we want for ourselves rather than for God.

Maybe we long to get married or have a baby. Maybe we prize a close friendship or a happy marriage or our children's success. Maybe we want job security or to grow a small business. Maybe personal fitness or getting the best education is what matters most to us. Or maybe our value is more general: we want to feel connected with others, we want to use our gifts and talents, we want to make a difference in the world. These are all good values. But if we become anxious, angry, or unhappy when we can't have or might lose what we value, this is usually a clue that we have bent this value toward ourselves. We want something for our own selfish delight and fulfillment rather than for God's glory. A good value has turned bad, and it's starting to smell.

But Scripture tells us to "no longer live for [ourselves] but for him who for [our] sake died and was raised" (2 Cor. 5:15). In other words, we should value everything for the sake of Christ. We should want our families, our careers, and our plans to bring glory to Christ above all. We should ask ourselves: Do I want my children to be successful for the honor of Christ? Do I want my marriage to represent Christ and his church? Do I want to grow my small business to serve others and glorify God? If our heart's desire is "that in everything God may be glorified through Jesus Christ" (1 Pet. 4:11), then our values will line up with Scripture, and the godly emotions of love, joy, and peace will expand in our hearts.

Christ is the greatest value of all. He alone is worthy of all glory (Rev. 5:12). But can we truly say, "There is nothing on earth that I desire besides you" (Ps. 73:25), or is there an asterisk next to "nothing"? If your honest answer to What do I *really* want? is anything other than Christ, then you have located your sinful value. But when you repent, discarding your sinful value for the "surpassing worth of knowing Christ Jesus" (Phil. 3:8), your emotions will be transformed. As John Piper says, "Being satisfied with all that God is for you in Jesus magnifies him as the greatest treasure and brings you more joy—eternal, infinite joy—than any other delight ever could."[4]

Growing in Godly Emotions

If you feel trapped in a tangled web of sinful emotions and don't know where to start, choose *one* sinful feeling. We cannot identify, catalog, and process all of our sinful beliefs and values at once. And we're not supposed to! Start small. Start with one. Choose one belief or value and prayerfully bring it to God's Word. Ask: *What one lie is feeding this emotion?* and *What selfish value is behind this feeling?*

Begin by confessing your sin to God (1 John 1:9). Ask for faith to overcome your sinful belief—"I believe; help my unbelief" (Mark 9:24), and for grace to put off your selfish value—"Incline my heart to your testimonies, and not to selfish gain!" (Ps. 119:36). Target your unbelief with the "precious and very great promises" of God (2 Pet. 1:4), and reorient your value by filling your mind with "the glory of our Lord Jesus Christ" (2 Thess. 2:14). When we take time each day to fill our minds with the truth and worth of Christ, we can expel our sinful beliefs and values. And, oh, happy discovery: change in one area affects every area of our lives.

There is hope and help for all of us in dealing with our emotions, including Charity, whom we met at the beginning of this chapter. We pray that God will restore Charity's relationship with her mother, but even if her mother never changes, Charity's emotions can change. She can learn how to relate to her mom without becoming bitter, frustrated, or upset. When Charity identifies her own sinful beliefs and values, and brings them to God's Word, her anger and bitterness will fade away, and feelings of love and compassion for her mom will spring up in their place. It probably won't happen overnight or in one phone call, but by the grace of God, it will happen. As Charity strives to grow, God's grace works to create godly emotions in her heart.

When we go after our sinful beliefs and values, our sinful emotions will recede. And one day we'll look back and realize: *I don't feel that way anymore.* Change doesn't happen overnight. Progress may be slow, and the more complicated or entrenched our sinful beliefs and values, the longer it may take. Growth in godly emotions, like growth in every area of our lives, comes, not in an instant, but over time. As the pastor and hymnwriter John Newton wrote:

> Remember, the growth of a believer is not like a mushroom, but like an oak, which increases slowly indeed but surely.

Many suns, showers, and frosts, pass upon it before it comes to perfection; and in the winter, when it seems dead, it is gathering strength at the root. Be humble, watchful, and diligent in the means, and endeavor to look through all, and fix your eye upon Jesus, and all shall be well.[5]

When we believe and value Christ above all, slowly but surely, our feelings will change. Through the Spirit's work in our hearts, we can feel what God wants us to feel.

7

Act to Feel

Like many young children, Nicole's son, Jack, used to have trouble pronouncing words with a *th* sound, and so he would say "I'm firsty" or "I lost a toof" or "I have firteen raisins." Even when Jack was old enough to know how these words were supposed to sound, he still couldn't pronounce them correctly. He needed to train his mouth to form the sound he wanted to say. Nicole looked online and found a speech therapist who suggested teaching children to stick out their tongues when saying *th* words. Jack had fun practicing: what child doesn't like to stick out his tongue? Soon he could properly pronounce thirsty, tooth, and thirteen.

Why did Jack have difficulty saying his *th* words correctly? Because he said them wrong for such a long time. In order to correct his speech, he had to develop a new habit. Why do we sometimes have difficulty dislodging our sinful beliefs and values? Why do we sometimes make so little progress cultivating obedient emotions? As we target our sinful beliefs and values with truth, our emotions don't always shift as quickly as we would like. That's because we may have reinforced our sinful beliefs and values through certain bad habits. As a result, our sinful beliefs and values become deeply embedded and resistant to change. David Powlison writes, "What we 'really believe' [and 'really want'] is not casually discarded or exchanged."[1] In order to correct our beliefs and values, we need to replace our bad habits with godly habits.

By the grace of God, we can put a stop to the bad habits of *thinking*, *saying*, and *doing,* and we can develop good habits that strengthen the truth and worth of Christ. Scripture calls this putting off and putting on (Eph. 4:20–24; Col. 3:9–14). When we put off old habits and put on new ones, even our most stubborn beliefs and values will shift and realign. As philosopher James K. A. Smith says, "We are creatures of habit . . . God knows this (since he created us), and thus our gracious, redeeming God meets us where we are by giving us Spirit-empowered, heart-calibrating, habit-forming practices to retrain our loves. This is the means of the Spirit's transformation."[2] The Holy Spirit helps us to put off bad habits that keep us stuck in sinful beliefs and values and put on new habits that retrain our emotions. We can approach the process of change with great hope, for our Creator is also our Helper (Ps. 54:4; 72:12). He knows us, and he meets us where we are.

Don't Ruminate; Meditate on Truth

What do you think about all day? Many of us get stuck in sinful thought patterns that reinforce the "lies and lusts" fueling our emotions.[3] Maybe we stew over someone's sin against us, or weave imaginary fearful scenarios, or brood about our sins and weaknesses. We ruminate. We curve in on ourselves. And ruminating on sinful thoughts is a bad habit that strengthens our sinful emotions. In fact, it is the opposite of obeying God with our emotions, because instead of moving toward God, we engage our emotions by ourselves, leaving God out of the process.

Now we can't just *stop* ruminating. Try it. It doesn't work. But we *can* replace this bad habit with the good habit of meditating on truth. "Whatever is true . . . think about these things" (Phil. 4:8). Find one truth to counteract a lie, and then think about it until it sticks. Replace a fearful scenario with a promise from Scripture. Instead of bitter ruminations, consider God's hatred of bitterness. Ponder the forgiveness of Christ rather than your failures. When we abandon our sinful ruminations for the truth of God's Word, the Holy Spirit will revitalize our emotions.

Take "mommy guilt" for example. How do we end up carrying the weight of this crushing emotion? And how can we get rid of it? Mommy guilt begins with a bad habit: ruminating on our sins and failures. Maybe we get angry at our children, but even after we repent and ask their forgiveness, we continue to berate ourselves. The more we review our failures, the more we believe we're terrible mothers, and the more guilty we feel.

Not only does ruminating on our sins lead to sinful emotions, it also dishonors our Savior who bore our sins for us. If we have confessed and repented, our sins are forgiven, forgotten, and far away: "There is therefore now no condemnation for those who are in Christ Jesus" (Rom. 8:1), and he has "cast all our sins into the depths of the sea" (Mic. 7:19). We should not think about our sins anymore but instead contemplate the Savior's sacrifice for our sins.

Or maybe we make a mommy-fail list in our heads, recounting all the ways we fall short: I should have played with my children more. I should have prepared healthier meals. I should have read more books aloud. The more we ruminate, the more we're convinced that we've messed up, and the worse our feelings of guilt become. To stop our guilty ruminations, maybe we should shut off the fount of extrabiblical parenting advice and focus solely on what God's Word says to parents. You see, Scripture's parenting guidelines aren't burdensome or complicated or always changing, and they come with the promise of God's help. "Bring them up in the discipline and instruction of the Lord" (Eph. 6:4), and "Train up a child in the way he should go; even when he is old he will not depart from it" (Prov. 22:6). When we fix our attention on God's standard, instead of fixating on what everyone else is doing, our beliefs will realign with God's truth, and we will begin to feel peace and hope.

Many of us also get caught in the sinful thought pattern of comparison. We measure and remeasure our beauty, accomplishments, possessions, and relationships against those of other people. Sometimes we come up short, sending our emotions into a tailspin of discontent. Other times, we think we have the edge and revel in an emotional glow of superiority. Either way, ruminating about ourselves *in comparison to others* reinforces our selfish values, inevitably leading to emotions of sinful discontent or delight.

Nicole has a friend who is a gifted writer, but her work is sometimes passed over in favor of younger, less-gifted writers. How does this friend stave off the temptations to self-pity or envy? She doesn't ruminate on what other women get or what she deserves, and she doesn't dwell on lies about God's character or dream about success. She even shut down one of her social media accounts because it tempted her to compare.

The gripping emotions of self-pity or self-satisfaction don't mysteriously sneak up on us. They come from a bad habit of comparison that nourishes our selfish values. We can break into our sinful thought patterns and remind ourselves of Jesus's counsel for Peter when he compared his situation to John's: "What is that to you? You follow me" (John 21:22). In other words, "It's none of your business. Don't even think about the other person. Follow me instead." When we contemplate how to follow Christ and serve others for Christ's sake, we won't have time to compare haves or have nots. Our selfish values will wither and die, and our smug or envious emotions will dissipate.

See how ruminating can be detrimental to our emotions? If we spend twenty minutes a day reading our Bibles, but the remaining twenty-three hours and forty minutes ruminating on unbiblical thoughts, then it is no wonder that our sinful beliefs and values are so stubborn and our sinful emotions so strong. Sinful ruminating can reverse the good effects of time spent in God's Word. It slows our growth and keeps us stuck in the same sinful emotions. We can't expect to grow godly emotions in the soil of our sinful ruminations, so if we struggle to change our beliefs and values, this bad habit is the place to start.

To kick the bad habit of sinful ruminating, we need a simple plan to redirect our thought patterns. Maybe we write down verses, memorize them, and review them often. Maybe we load sermons or worship songs and hymns on our mobile devices. If need be, we can even ask our husbands or friends to remind us of truth on a daily basis. We have to be deliberate, and we have to persist. But if we meditate on what is true, lovely, and admirable—all day long—we will cultivate godly beliefs and values from which obedient emotions will flourish (Phil. 4:8).

Don't Vent; Pour Out Your Soul to God

We usually feel better after we vent our emotions. For a moment, anyway. We get whatever's bothering us off our chests. We feel an immediate release from the emotional pressure building up inside. But venting doesn't purge our systems of sinful emotions; it ties the knot of sinful beliefs and values tighter around our hearts. Every time we verbalize our lies and lusts, we strengthen their grip, whether yelling in anger or muttering complaints, whether uttering our gripes with our mouths or typing them into our keyboards. Scripture tells us, "A fool gives full vent to his spirit, but a wise man quietly holds it back" (Prov. 29:11). Venting is foolish; it dishonors God and often hurts those we love the most. Even though we feel sorry after we vent, many of us revert to this bad habit. But if it's wrong to vent, how do we handle our tumultuous feelings? To answer this question, let's consider the story of Hannah in the Bible.

Hannah had every reason to vent her emotions. You only have to read the first two verses of 1 Samuel 1 to understand why. "There was a certain man . . . whose name was Elkanah. . . . He had two wives. The name of the one was Hannah, and the name of the other, Peninnah. And Peninnah had children, but Hannah had no children" (vv. 1–2). To make matters worse for Hannah, "her rival [Peninnah] used to provoke her grievously to irritate her" (v. 6). Hannah could not stop crying, and she would not eat (v. 7). She was in the depths of despair.

And yet, we find no record in Scripture of Hannah venting anger or self-pity to her husband or anyone else. Instead, Hannah cried out to God in her emotional distress. She "prayed to the LORD and wept bitterly" (1 Sam. 1:10). She opened the floodgates of her soul before the Lord, and, as Charles Spurgeon put it, "Turn[ed] the vessel of [her] soul upside down in [God's] secret presence, and let [her] inmost thoughts, desires, sorrows, and sins be poured out like water."[4]

Hannah's prayer was an honest, fervent, "meet God where you are" kind of prayer. There were tears with this prayer, lots of tears. "Sometimes tears themselves apparently constitute prayer, for the Lord hears 'the sound of [our] weeping' (Ps. 6:8)."[5] As the tears spilled out, Hannah spilled out her soul to the Lord. In fact, when Eli, the high priest, confronted Hannah and accused her of being drunk, she told him that she was praying out of her great emotion. "I am a woman troubled in spirit. I have drunk neither wine nor strong drink, but I have been pouring out my soul before the LORD. Do not regard your servant as a worthless woman, for all along I have been speaking out of my great anxiety and vexation" (1 Sam. 1:15–16). Hannah was not concerned with maintaining a stoic facade for Eli or anyone else, but neither did she vent her emotions to anyone who would listen. Like a wise woman, she held back her feelings until she could pour them out before the Lord. Following Hannah's example, we should freely pour out our emotions to God in prayer.

God created emotions so we could express them to him. He doesn't expect us to keep them all pent up. But neither does he want us to pour them out before other people in gossip, slander, or complaining. Sadly, the first instinct of many women is to vent their emotions on social media instead of pouring out their hearts to God. Women often vent to online friends and find comfort and solace in each other's "likes" and reassuring comments. And while it is true that God encourages us to share our burdens, including our emotional burdens, with other Christians, this is not a license to sinfully vent. There's a world of difference between spewing our sinful emotions and asking for help from other Christians. So instead of resorting to the bad habit of venting, let's ask a friend, Will you help me take my emotions to the Lord?

Hannah poured out her soul before the Lord, and the Lord

rescued Hannah from her emotional distress. When Hannah rose and left the temple, she was still barren. She was still the shamed woman in a polygamous marriage. But her emotions had changed: "her face was no longer sad" (1 Sam. 1:18). She was filled with peaceful, even happy, emotions, and it showed on her face and in her demeanor. We know the end of Hannah's story. God not only changed her emotions but he also changed her situation. He gave her a son, Samuel, whom she gave back to the Lord. The full effect of Hannah's transformed emotions is on display in the second chapter of first Samuel, where she sings a hymn of praise to God: "My heart exults in the LORD. . . . He raises up the poor from the dust; he lifts the needy from the ash heap" (1 Sam. 2:1, 8). Hannah's heart exulted in the Lord. Her emotions moved her to worship God. While venting fortifies our sinful beliefs and values, when we pour out our souls to the Lord, he lifts our burdens and restores our emotions.

Don't Wait to Feel; Act to Feel

When the girls were young, dinnertime rules in the Mahaney home were simple: no elbows on the table, chew with your mouth closed, and eat at least one bite of whatever was being served. The last one was the hardest. Many a night, Nicole would sit staring at a single bite of food on her plate. The longer she sat, the less she felt like eating. Eventually, she would choke it down with a glass of water, but it was always worse for the waiting.

Emotions work the same way. If we delay or avoid acts of

obedience because we "don't feel like it," the more we won't feel like it. The longer we go without reading our Bibles, the less we want to read them. The more serving opportunities we pass up, the less we feel like serving, and the more times we skip church, the less we feel like going. If we procrastinate in our work, we feel less inclined to finish it. That's because our faculties work together, and our actions (or inaction) affect how we feel. Waiting to feel before we act in obedience is a bad habit that bolsters our sinful emotions. Sinful beliefs and values only get stronger when we indulge our sinful feelings.

Instead of waiting to feel, we can act to feel. We can make choices and take actions that move us toward God and others in obedience, whether we feel like it at first or not. We can bring the faculty of the will to bear on the emotions. "In other words, if you want to encourage an emotion," writes professor Robert Campbell Roberts, "act in conformity with it, even if you don't initially feel like it."[6] For example, all those "one bites" paid off for Nicole. Because she learned to eat foods she didn't like, Nicole learned to like many foods. In the same way, our actions change our emotions. As counselor Mike Emlet puts it, "In carrying out a godly act, a godly desire can deepen."[7] If we act like we want to feel—in obedience to God—we will eventually feel the obedient emotions he calls us to feel.

For example, we may not feel like having that new family at church over for a meal, but when we do (in spite of our selfish feelings), we enjoy fellowship and maybe even make new friends. The more we *show* love to others, the more we will *feel* love for others. Our actions realign our beliefs and values—and change our emotions. Parents can teach children to "act to feel" at a young age. Put on a smile. Share a toy. Do your homework, whether you feel like it or not. And you know what? You will feel better after a while. Act obedient to feel obedient. Many parents worry that requiring their children to follow rules will produce little legalists. But the opposite is true. When we follow Scripture's parenting guidelines and teach our children to act in obedience—whether they feel like it or not—we create the ideal context for good and happy emotions to flourish.

Carolyn once heard a man say that the best advice his dad ever gave him was, "If you want to be in a better mood, act like you are." The man remembered how phony this advice seemed to him at first, but as he got older, he learned that it was true. If you act better than you feel, you will feel better. Far from being fake or phony, acting to feel is biblical. We find one vivid account in the book of Isaiah. God's people were acting wickedly, and so God commanded them to put on acts of righteousness instead. He promised that if they acted in obedience, they would experience new and glorious emotions:

> If you pour yourself out for the hungry
>   and satisfy the desire of the afflicted,
> then shall your light rise in the darkness
>   and your gloom be as the noonday.
> And the LORD will guide you continually
>   and satisfy your desire in scorched places.
>   (Isa. 58:10–11)

What acts of love and care for others have we been putting off until we feel like it? Instead of repeating the bad habit of waiting to feel, let's act to feel. Then we, too, will find that our gloom has lifted and our desires are richly satisfied by the grace of God.

"The Best Kind of Progress"

When a sinful emotion "clings so closely" (Heb. 12:1), we might be tempted to think that our beliefs and values are too strong after all, that real change isn't possible. But to believe this is to fall prey to another one of Satan's lies. The truth is that "it is God who works in you, both to will and to work for his good pleasure" (Phil. 2:13). Even when we don't see it, even when we don't *feel* it, God is lovingly at work in our lives through the power of the Holy Spirit to help us dislodge sinful beliefs and values and change our emotions. Elizabeth Prentiss, author of the hymn "More Love to Thee," once wrote to a friend:

> God never places us in any position in which we can not grow. We may fancy that He does. We may fear we are so impeded by fretting, petty cares that we are gaining nothing; but when we are not sending any branches upward, we may be sending roots downward. Perhaps in the time of our humiliation, when everything seems a failure, we are making the best kind of progress.[8]

Even when everything seems like a failure, God is helping us to make progress toward emotional obedience. "He who began a good work in you will bring it to completion at the day of Jesus Christ" (Phil. 1:6). Yes, we must work to put off bad habits of thinking, saying, and doing, and to obey Christ with our emotions, but our hope is not ultimately in our own abilities. Our hope is in Christ, who started this good work in the first place. He is at work, right now, creating godly emotions in our hearts, and he won't stop until our lives are bursting with beautiful, passionate, true feelings.

8

God's Purpose in Pain

One sunny, summer day last year, a young father in our church lost his life in a car accident. He was on his way to work when another car drove through a stop sign and into the side of his vehicle. His death was sudden, and it was horrible. He left behind a young wife, three small girls, and a son born just eight days after he went to be with the Lord. One Sunday he was at church with us, and the next Sunday he was gone. We were all shocked and grief-stricken. We're still grieving. Even as we weep with his widow, our dear friend, we cannot begin to understand her emotions of grief. Maybe you understand. Tragedy and loss have hurled you into a new emotional universe where every feeling has coalesced into a single, unrelenting, searing pain. As far as you can see, there is nothing but pain, and you wonder if you will ever feel happy again.

Another dear friend of ours is a mother who has a demanding little boy. Her life feels overshadowed by his disobedience.

She awakens each morning, dreading a long day of training and discipline, and she goes to bed each night wondering if she's made any progress at all. Sometimes the only movement seems to be backward. She has worked faithfully to honor God by teaching and correcting her son, but the trial of his disobedience seems interminable. Even though she has a wonderful husband and three other delightful children, this one child's behavior dominates her emotional life, dragging it down. Dread in the morning, unhappiness during the day, discouragement in the evening. Like so many of you, she is not dealing with heartbreak, but with heartache—with the steady, unrelenting drip of painful, unpleasant emotions.

Our friend with the difficult son would never compare her unhappy emotions to our friend who lost her husband, and neither do we. But heartache and heartbreak both raise the question: *How do we deal with painful emotions?* What does emotional obedience look like in the agony of loss or in the angst of a losing battle? What are we supposed to do with the air-sucking, soul-piercing feelings of grief or the constant, strength-sapping feelings of discouragement?

How do we deal with the excruciating pain when a husband betrays the marriage or a parent is diagnosed with Alzheimer's, when a friendship is broken beyond repair or an illness drags on for years, when a loved one dies or an unborn baby's heartbeat goes silent? And how do we deal with the everyday pain when a marriage is struggling or a friendship is contentious, when a child is rebellious or a family relationship is strained, when debt is mounting or PMS is severe? We feel at a loss. We simply do not know what to do. The pain is overwhelming.

Chances are, you picked up this book because you want to know how to deal with difficult emotions. You are not skipping from rock to rock of happy feelings like a little girl crossing a creek on a sunny day. No matter where you step, you land on a slippery stone of sadness or a jagged rock of anxiety and lose your emotional balance. Or maybe you're drowning in the rip currents of agonizing emotions. When it comes to our emotions, many of us feel like we're going from sadness to sadness instead of "from strength to strength" (Ps. 84:7). We want to obey, but we don't know what to do when difficult feelings engulf our lives. Can we change our painful emotions? Can we do away with all the hurt and depression that we feel? Or should we embrace our grief and feel it deeply? How do we handle painful feelings?

Painful Emotions: As Unsurprising as They Are Unpleasant

As Christians, we often feel ashamed of our painful feelings. Maybe we are concerned that other Christians will think we are weak and immature if we appear unhappy, so we hide our pain and pretend we are full of faith. We worry that we are not trusting God or that we must be sinning in some way if we feel sad. If we struggle with depression, we think we must be a failure as a Christian. If we feel blue or fretful during PMS, we believe God is displeased with us. Our confusion produces condemnation and despair, which only leads to deeper pain.

In fact, painful emotions are often the reason we wish we could get rid of emotions altogether. We would happily give up pleasant feelings if only we didn't have to deal with misery and sadness. As Dan Allender and Tremper Longman explain:

> The reason we don't want to feel is that feeling exposes the tragedy of our world and the darkness of our hearts . . . feelings expose the illusion that life is safe, good, and predictable . . . it's painful to feel. To feel hurt, hurts. To feel shame, shames. To feel any loss only intensifies sorrow. . . . All of us prefer to avoid pain—but even more, we want to escape reality.[1]

Because pain is so hard to feel, we often suppress our grief and sorrow. We would rather deny reality than feel it. We avoid people who are in pain, and we try to avoid our own pain. We dive into a world of distractions where reality is shallow and safe. We did not expect the Christian life to be full of so much pain and sadness.

But Scripture tells us that painful feelings are a fact of life. They are normal for the Christian. As David Powlison says, "Many people do not know that it is legitimate to experience hardship, pain, and temptation."[2] And nowhere does Scripture say that we will be immune to difficult emotions. Quite the opposite. From the moment sin entered the world, God's people have known sadness, hurt, anxiety, misery, and agony. Jesus promised his followers that "in this world you will have trouble" (John 16:33 NIV), and trouble generates troubling emotions. The Christian is often "grieved by various trials"

(1 Pet. 1:6). You cannot go far in Scripture without bumping into sorrow:

- "Why are you cast down, O my soul, and why are you in turmoil within me?" cried the psalmist (Ps. 42:5).
- "My soul is bereft of peace; I have forgotten what happiness is," declared the man of God (Lam. 3:17).
- "A voice is heard in Ramah, lamentation and bitter weeping," foretold the prophet (Jer. 31:15).
- "We ourselves . . . groan inwardly as we wait," lamented the saints (Rom. 8:23).
- "I have great sorrow and unceasing anguish in my heart," wrote the apostle (Rom. 9:2).

The Psalms include almost twice as many songs of lament as hymns of praise or thanksgiving, and there is even a book of the Bible entitled "Lamentations." Perhaps, most remarkable of all, our Lord and Savior chooses to be identified using the language of painful emotions: "a man of sorrows" (Isa. 53:3). "You are not the first child of God who has been depressed or troubled," wrote Charles Spurgeon, for "among the noblest of men and women who ever lived, there has been much of this kind of thing. . . . Do not, therefore, think that you are quite alone in your sorrow."[3]

We are not alone in our pain, and neither should we feel guilty or ashamed. Tim Keller illustrates from the life of Job: "Here is a man already behaving in a way that many pious Christians would consider at least unseemly or showing a lack of faith. He rips his clothes, falls to the ground, cries out. He does not show any stoical patience. But the biblical text says,

'In all this Job sinned not.'"[4] Job did not suppress his painful emotions, but freely expressed his grief for all to see.

What's "unnatural," Martyn Lloyd-Jones explained, are not Christians who grieve, but Christians who deny the reality of sorrow and grief; this "goes beyond the New Testament [and] . . . savours more of the stoic or of the psychological state produced by a cult rather than of Christianity."[5] Grief and sorrow are normal for the Christian. What's more, they are glorious—for through our sorrows we have the opportunity to share in the sufferings of our Savior (2 Cor. 1:5).

How Painful Emotions Tell and Move

Like all our emotions, painful emotions tell and move. Sometimes we have yucky emotions that simply tell us our bodies are out of sorts due to hormones, illness, or the side effects of medication. But most of the time, our painful emotions tell us that something we value is threatened, lost, or out of reach, or that something we believe in or hope for may never come to pass. For example, if you value your job and get demoted, or make a close friend and she moves away, or if you watch your child get hurt, you experience fear and sadness. Or if you believe God led you to a church but it splits, or that God was going to heal you but you don't get better, you feel discouraged. In all these cases, our painful emotions are, as Mark Talbot says, "reacting against something;" they rise up against whatever endangers our values and beliefs.[6]

When our painful emotions oppose what God says is wrong with this world, they are right and godly. When our friend who lost her husband experiences soul-shaking grief, anger, and hurt, her emotions reflect something true about God: he hates death. Our Savior was "deeply moved"—indignant and outraged—at the death of his friend Lazarus (John 11:33). And "Jesus wept" with compassion, even though he knew he would shortly raise Lazarus from the dead (John 11:35). The shortest verse in the Bible is full of our Savior's anguish and sorrow over what's wrong with the world.

Painful emotions are right when they rise up against everyday wrongs, too. It is right to feel grieved if your child disobeys. It is right to feel angry if a coworker gossips. It is right to feel sorrow if your church breaks into factions. It is right to feel that a wrong against God is wrong.

Our painful feelings should also move us to cry out to God for help. Sadly, we often ignore God until we feel painful emotions. When we are drifting along on calm seas and under sunny skies, we don't feel our need for God, but as soon as painful emotions surface, we feel desperate and weak, and these emotions should move us to God. As C. S. Lewis famously observed in his book, *The Problem of Pain*, "We can ignore even pleasure. But pain insists on being attended to. God whispers to us in our pleasures, speaks in our conscience, but shouts in our pain: it is His megaphone to rouse a deaf world."[7]

Feelings of unhappiness, despair, anxiety, guilt, and grief are meant to perform a fruitful function in our lives. They are supposed to move us to God. "Before I was afflicted I went astray," said the psalmist, "but now I keep your word" (Ps.

119:67). As Powlison puts it, "When you let life's troubles get to you, it gets you to the only one who can help."[8] The discouragement of failing an exam, the soul-weariness of motherhood, the anxiety over finances, the anger at someone mistreating your child, even the agony of losing a loved one—all of these painful emotions are intended to get us to the only one who can help.

Here we make a surprising discovery: the emotions we need rescuing from may also be the emotions that move us to safety. If we cry out to God, instead of denying or ignoring our pain, then, in one sense, we are already in the rescue boat. That's because what we need, more than a fix for our emotions, is God himself. Our emotional rip currents are often the force that pushes us to cry out to God when nothing else will. As Joni Eareckson Tada—whose diving accident in 1967 left her a quadriplegic in a wheelchair—insightfully shares, "Rather than try to frantically escape the pain, I relearned the timeless lesson of allowing my suffering to push me deeper into the arms of Jesus. I like to think of my pain as a sheepdog that keeps snapping at my heels to drive me down the road to Calvary, where, otherwise, I would not be naturally inclined to go."[9] Painful emotions are intended to drive us to our Savior.

Telling Emotional Time

Scripture tells us that there is a time for painful emotions:

> There is . . .
> a time to weep, and a time to laugh;
> a time to mourn, and a time to dance. (Eccles. 3:1, 4)

If, in fact, there is a time for weeping and mourning, then we need to know what time that is. As Christians, we need to learn how to tell emotional time. We need to understand *when* it is time for groaning or sighing, and *how long* we should expect painful emotions to last. Is it OK that I cry in the bathroom because my work environment is so stressful? Is it wrong that I still grieve the loss of my husband, even after all these years? Am I a bad mother because I don't always enjoy my children? Am I weak and immature because I suffer from postpartum depression?

Like a fingerprint, no two experiences of pain are alike. Even if we "share Christ's sufferings" (1 Pet. 4:13) along with other Christians, we do not share identical experiences of suffering. Because we all have different beliefs and values, and because these beliefs and values interact with our life circumstances in an infinite variety of ways, we all have different experiences of pain. We know that pain should move us to God and godliness, but what does it look like for each one of us? To find the answer, we need to set our emotional watches to biblical time.

When we experience a severe tragedy or trauma, painful emotions remain for a long while. We cannot expect these strong emotions to evaporate quickly. If your husband leaves you or you are slandered, if you have a miscarriage or if you are abused, if death casts its shadow over your home, the pain will be intense and enduring. "Believers can stay in darkness for a long time," writes Keller.[10] Thus the psalmist's refrain,

"How long, O LORD?" (Ps. 13:1). Pain is not in a hurry to leave. Grief outstays its welcome.

For example, when we read the book of Job, we may wonder: Why is it so long? Why so many chapters of agony and arguments? Why do we have to listen to Eliphaz drone on while Job rubs his sores? "Job cannot be distilled," insists commentator Christopher Ash. "It is a narrative with a very slow pace (after the frenetic beginning) and long delays. Why? Because there is no instant working through grief, no quick fix to pain, no message of Job in a nutshell. God has given us a forty-two chapter journey with no satisfactory bypass."[11] God did not restore Job after a few minutes of pain, and if our grief and sorrow go on for a long time, we should take our place next to Job, and patiently cry out to God.

Pain may come suddenly and stay for a long time. God does not rush us through the experience of pain and heartbreak, even if sometimes that's what it feels like other people try to do. "We can so super-spiritualize the Christian life that we do not leave room for the times of deep, painful, faith-shaking affliction," observes Brian Borgman.[12] Job's friends were impatient for a resolution to his problems, and often we feel like other people are impatient for us to move on or put our pain behind us. "There is seldom a place provided for lamentation in the church, and down to the present day, many do not give sufferers the freedom to weep," Keller says.[13]

God not only gives us time to weep, but, as we are told in Isaiah, "in all [our] affliction he [is] afflicted" (63:9). We do not know how long our painful emotions will last, but we know that God has them perfectly timed. This is our comfort: they will not last one minute longer than he ordains. As we move toward God in our sorrows, "joy comes with the morning" (Ps. 30:5).

But what about everyday trials—the setbacks and discouragements, the heartache and weariness of daily life—how do we deal with these difficult emotions? Even if our initial responses are legitimate and godly, we are all tempted to make our painful emotions more about us than about God. We need to learn how to tell emotional time in the bumps and bruises of daily life.

When little trials go on and on, they begin to feel like big trials. And at some point, we're all tempted to get more upset about how the trouble is affecting us and less concerned about how we are honoring God. But there's a difference between sitting quietly in a season of darkness and curling up into a ball of self-pity because we don't get what we want. Painful emotions may be right, but given the reality of indwelling sin, we also need to be on the lookout for when they turn wrong.

To tell proper time, we need to ask what our painful emotions are telling us. What is it that our painful emotions are opposing right now? Are they rising up against something that obscures God's glory or something that injures our pride? Are we resisting sin or the loss of our own comfort? Are we saddened by something that offends God or something that offends us? Are we indignant because God's law is being broken or because our own "rights" are being violated? We need to distinguish between a season of suffering and a self-induced pity party.

The key question is: Are my painful emotions moving me toward God or toward myself? The answer to this question will unlock the truth about our painful feelings.

The Joyful Gift of Painful Emotions

So how do we deal with painful emotions? Scripture tells us. Difficult, even agonizing emotions are normal for the Christian, and they are intended to move us to God. We need to be women who learn to tell good emotional time. When do we need to wait patiently on God in the midst of painful emotions, and when do we need to move toward God in repentance because our painful emotions have turned selfish? Keller answers:

> When you are not all absorbed in yourself, you can feel the sadness of the world. And therefore, what you actually have is that the joy of the Lord happens inside the sorrow. It doesn't come after the sorrow. It doesn't come after the uncontrollable weeping. The weeping drives you into the joy, it enhances the joy, and then the joy enables you to actually feel your grief without its sinking you. In other words, you are finally emotionally healthy.[14]

The weeping drives you into the joy. Painful emotions that move us to God invariably move us to joy. The "God of all comfort" (2 Cor. 1:3) is also the One in whose presence we find "fullness of joy" (Ps. 16:11). Joy does not necessarily displace sorrow; one of the mysteries of the Christian life is that we may experience genuine joy alongside searing pain. Whether in life-shattering trials or workaday troubles, we must move to God in our painful emotions. God does not want us to avoid the painful realities of a sin-soaked world; neither does he permit us to give in to our selfish desires. When we turn away from ourselves and move toward God, and when we relentlessly seek God in our trouble, we will know the miraculous comingling of pain and joy, grief and gladness, sorrow and delight. We will learn what it means to be "sorrowful, yet always rejoicing" (2 Cor. 6:10).

"Happy storm that wrecks a man on such a rock as this!" wrote Spurgeon:

> O blessed hurricane that drives the soul to God and God alone! . . . When a man is so poor, so friendless, so helpless that he has nowhere else to turn, he flies into his Father's arms, and is blessedly clasped therein! When he is burdened with troubles so pressing and so peculiar, that he cannot tell them to any but his God, he may be thankful for them; for he will learn more of his Lord than at any other time. Oh, tempest-tossed believer, it is a happy trouble that drives thee to thy Father![15]

Painful feelings, no matter how unpleasant, are a "happy trouble" when they drive us to a deeper knowledge and fellowship with our suffering Savior.

9

Godly Emotions for Life

In J. R. R. Tolkien's *Lord of the Rings* trilogy, the young hobbit Pippin observes a depth and range of emotions in the face of the ancient wizard Gandalf: "Pippin glanced in some wonder at the face now close beside his own. . . . He saw at first only lines of care and sorrow; though as he looked more intently he perceived that under all there was a great joy: a fountain of mirth enough to set a kingdom laughing, were it to gush forth."[1] In Gandalf—and in other Tolkien characters such as Treebeard and the elves—we see what Ralph C. Wood calls "the essential Tolkienian demeanor—a fundamental somberness about the world's state, yet with an overriding joy that cannot be quenched."[2]

What Pippin saw in Gandalf also describes the essential *Christian* demeanor: our emotions should tell, in deep and profound ways, of both the sadness of this fallen world and the joy of the gospel. The mature emotional Christian is not happy all the time; she is not an annoyingly upbeat, "always turning lemons into lemonade" kind of person. The emotional character we are striving for is multifaceted, reflecting a full range of godly emotions: from sincere grief over sin to earnest hope for heaven, from righteous anger at injustice to genuine affection for our fellow man. We are to be, as Tolkien said, "sad, but not unhappy,"[3] and as the apostle Paul described, "sorrowful, yet always rejoicing" (2 Cor. 6:10). How do we get like this? What will it take to attain an emotional demeanor that is "somber" about life in this fallen world, but saturated with "an overriding joy"? In this final chapter, we want to highlight God's means of grace that help us toward enduring Christian maturity.

We see the full range of human emotions most beautifully and perfectly displayed when we look at Jesus Christ. Our Savior's chief mission on earth was to seek and save the lost, and one of the fruits of his saving mission is that God is now at work conforming us to the image of his Son, including our emotions. "For those whom he foreknew he also predestined to be conformed to the image of his Son" (Rom. 8:29). Christlike emotions are what we're destined for, but it is also a goal we must work toward (Col. 1:29). As Christians, we must actively cultivate Christlike emotions in our lives. And to do that, we must look to Christ; we must focus on the image of God's Son to whom we are being conformed.

The Measure of Emotional Maturity

The next time you read through the Gospels, look for how often Jesus's emotions were the exact opposite of everyone around him. You will see that our Lord's emotions were almost always surprising and unexpected. When the disciples tried to keep the children from coming to Jesus, "he was indignant and said to them, 'Let the children come to me'" (Mark 10:14). While the average Jewish citizen was untroubled by the merchants and money-changers in the temple, Jesus overturned their tables and drove them out with whips because of his "zeal for [his Father's] house" (John 2:17). Perhaps most stunning of all, we see our Lord's thankfulness as he offered up the bread and wine at the Last Supper, symbols of his death and suffering (Luke 22:19–20).

The reason for Jesus's radically different emotions was their object: to please his heavenly Father. Jesus loved to do his Father's will, was angry at whatever offended his Father, and perfectly reflected his Father's mercy. "We see in Jesus the most exquisite blend of compassion, sympathy, pain, frustration and anger in one whose mind and heart were in perfect harmony with his Father's," wrote Clifford Pond.[4] What about our emotions—are they in harmony with God's mind and heart? Is their object the glory of God? Godly emotions will be in tune with pleasing God, which means they will frequently surprise the world around us.

Many people assume that emotional maturity means fewer highs and fewer lows, that our goal is to feel *less* rather than more. But when we look at Jesus's emotions, we see that he was a man of deep, intense feeling. He was "deeply moved" (John 11:33), and he "earnestly desired" (Luke 22:15); he was "very sorrowful" (Matt. 26:38) and "full of joy" (Luke 10:21 NIV).

Jesus did not attempt to hide his strong emotions. He prayed "with loud cries and tears" (Heb. 5:7) and, as B. B. Warfield described, displayed "open exultation of joy."[5] The more Christlike our emotions become, therefore, the more deeply we will feel: we'll experience deeper love for our fellow Christians, greater hatred of evil, stronger pity and compassion for sinners who are perishing, and more fervent joy in the Lord. So ask yourself: Do I feel more deeply about the things of God than ever before? How we answer is a measure of our emotional maturity.

Finally, Jesus's emotions always moved him to action. He "had compassion" (Matt. 14:14) on the crowds, and so he fed them. He felt "pity" (Matt. 20:34) for the two blind men, and so he restored their sight. Most profoundly of all, Jesus, "for the joy that was set before him endured the cross" (Heb. 12:2). Sometimes we feel right emotions—perhaps when we read God's Word each morning or listen to the sermon on Sunday—and we allow the feelings to wash over us and fade away. But our godly feelings are intended to move us to action. Compassion for others should overflow into acts of generosity. Love for our brothers and sisters in Christ should move us to pray for them. Grief over our sin should lead us to repent.

We observe in our Lord the glorious panorama of sinless human emotions (e.g., Matt. 8:10; Mark 3:5; Luke 10:21). As we consider our Savior's emotions, we see where we fall short, for sure; but we also see the beauty of what we are striving for and what we are being changed into: deeply intense emotions that are in harmony with God's will and move us to godly action. Most wonderful of all, when we look to Christ, our Savior, we are being changed. "And we all, with unveiled face, beholding the glory of the Lord, are being transformed into the same image from one degree of glory to another" (2 Cor. 3:18).

The Means of Emotional Maturity

By the grace of God, the scenery of our emotional lives can be full of true, deep, compelling emotions, like those of Christ. Through the power of his Holy Spirit, he works Christlike emotions in us through means of grace: Scripture, prayer, his church, and every good gift. As we make use of these means of grace, we will grow in mature, godly emotions.

SCRIPTURE AND PRAYER

Scripture has been written to implant, renew, and revive godly affections and emotions in our hearts. John Piper writes, "The divine fingers of Scripture are meant to pluck every string in the harp of your soul."[6] We're so used to being told that we should read Scripture *regardless* of how we feel, and this is true, but the end goal is not to check another box off our Bible reading plans. Instead, as we come to God's Word, feeling an emotional flatline, we can expect his Word to spark fresh feelings in our hearts. "The law of the LORD is perfect, reviving the soul . . . the precepts of the LORD are right, rejoicing the heart" (Ps. 19:7–8).

So, as the saying goes, let us "take up and read" to feel. George Müeller, eighteenth-century pastor and benefactor of orphans, described the transformative power that reading God's Word every day had upon his soul:

> For the first four years after my conversion I made no prog-
> ress, because I neglected the Bible. But when I regularly read
> on through the whole with reference to my own heart and
> soul, I directly made progress. Then my peace and joy con-
> tinued more and more. Now I have been doing this for 47
> years. I have read through the whole Bible about 100 times
> and I always find it fresh when I begin again. Thus my peace
> and joy have increased more and more.[7]

If we want our peace and joy to increase more and more, then we must regularly read our Bibles. As George Müeller learned from experience, the simple reason we often lack Christlike emotions is that we neglect the refreshing fountain of Scripture's truth. Often, we spend our emotional energy on trivialities like Facebook, football, or the Food Network, leaving our souls drained and dry. But Christlike emotions don't blossom without consistent nourishment from the Word of God.

Some days, when we read Scripture, our emotions are im-mediately revived; we wonder why we ever neglected to read God's Word in the first place. But other times—and we all know what this is like, too—we come to Scripture eager for emotional renewal, and feel like we come away empty. And so we should not only *read to feel*; we should *read until we feel* (Ps. 62:5). This does not mean that we stay in our quiet times in front of our Bibles, calling in sick to work or neglecting to care for our children until our emotions change. Rather, we must persevere in reading, never giving up, until, by the grace of God, we receive Christlike emotions. For as Martyn Lloyd-Jones wrote, "to see the truth means that you are moved by it and that you love it. You cannot help it. If you see the truth clearly, you must feel it."[8]

Prayer is also a primary way that God changes our emotions. Prayer is sometimes one of the last things we *feel* like doing, but our lack of feeling is the very reason we need to pray! Jesus told us to pray in order to feel: "Ask, and you will receive, that your joy may be full" (John 16:24). Through prayer we have access to the one person who can change our emotions. And when we ask, he does just that. Consider the testimony of the Psalms, an entire book of emotional prayers: "I sought the LORD, and he answered me and delivered me from all my fears" (Ps. 34:4), and "Out of my distress I called on the LORD; the LORD answered me and set me free" (Ps. 118:5), and "On the day I called, you answered me; my strength of soul you increased" (Ps. 138:3).

When we pray, we can unburden ourselves of every painful emotion. But more than that, we can get our emotions renewed and reshaped to be like Christ's. Prayer increases our love for what God loves and our hatred of what God hates. When we pray God's promises and truth back to him, our beliefs and values are changed, and our souls are filled with Christlike emotions. Brian Borgman explains:

> Prayer reflects our values and beliefs but it should also be shaping our values and beliefs. As we enter into the place of secret prayer we are not only pouring out our hearts; our

hearts are being shaped by God-centered goals and Christ-exalting values. The Holy Spirit takes those moments to cultivate more godly emotions in us. Prayer expresses, excites, and increases godly emotions.[9]

Again, George Müeller illustrates how prayer kindles godly emotions: "When thus I have been for awhile making confession, or intercession, or supplication, or have given thanks . . . the result of this is . . . that my inner man almost invariably is even sensibly nourished and strengthened, and that by breakfast time, with rare exceptions, I am in a peaceful if not happy state of heart."[10]

How would you describe your morning emotions? Are you in "a peaceful if not happy state of heart" by breakfast? Many mornings we wake to heavy sorrows and fresh anxieties, and no doubt, Müeller had plenty of both! But by breakfast time his emotions were often peaceful and happy, and ours can be as well. "Prayer *does* change things, all kinds of things," insists R. C. Sproul. "But the most important thing it changes is us. . . . Prayer changes us profoundly."[11] Prayer changes our emotions, and so we should pray to feel.

THE GATHERED CHURCH

We don't often connect church with emotions (unless it's how we don't feel like going), but one of the main reasons we should go to church each Sunday for worship, preaching, and fellowship is to refresh and revive Christlike emotions in our lives. "And let us consider how to stir up one another to love and good works, not neglecting to meet together, as is the habit of some, but encouraging one another, and all the more as you see the Day drawing near" (Heb. 10:24–25). We go to church to "stir up" in one another godly emotions such as "love," which move us to godly actions: "good works."

And our emotions desperately need to be stirred up. Think of your typical week, with all its challenges, temptations, responsibilities, setbacks, and sufferings. Each Sunday, we need to recover from the week before and prepare for what's ahead. "We are not refugees who are looking for escape; rather, we are wounded and weary soldiers who need rest and rehabilitation so we can go back into the battle," writes author Warren Wiersbe. Our experience at church "should lead to personal enrichment and enablement, the kind of spiritual strength that helps the believer carry the burdens and fight the battles of life."[12]

Why does God call us to sing "psalms and hymns and spiritual songs" when we gather together (Eph. 5:19)? Why do we not only speak the truth but also sing the truth? As Jonathan Edwards put it, "The duty of *singing* praises to God, seems to be appointed wholly to excite and express religious affections. No other reason can be assigned, why we should express ourselves to God in verse, rather than in prose, and do it with music, but only, that such is our nature and frame, that these things have a tendency to move our affections."[13] In other words, God created music for this purpose: to stir up our emotions for God and express our affections to God. This is why we worship.

Many of us think of preaching as the cerebral portion of

the meeting, but the true intent of preaching is also to stir up our emotions for God. Lloyd-Jones asked:

> Can a man see himself as a damned sinner without emotion? Can a man look into hell without emotion? Can a man listen to the thunderings of the Law and feel nothing? Or conversely, can a man really contemplate the love of God in Christ Jesus and feel no emotion? . . . This element of being moved, should always be prominent in preaching.[14]

So often, we ask our children, "What did you *learn* from the sermon?" but we don't usually ask, "What did you *feel* during the sermon?" The answer to this question may tell us more about the state of our children's souls and point all of us to a primary goal of listening to God's Word preached. The reason, said Edwards, for why "God hath appointed a particular and lively application of his word" is to raise our affections for Christ.[15]

The emotional effects of worship and preaching spill over into our fellowship with one another. We do church *together*, the book of Hebrews tells us, so that we can be "encouraging one another." Fellowship with other Christians on Sunday and throughout the week is a main and vital source of emotional sustenance. J. I. Packer writes, "Through fellowship, one's soul is refreshed and fed. . . . To have God's children praying for you, caring for you as a fellow-believer, and sharing their experiences of trial and triumph with you brings vast enrichment."[16] Our emotions are profoundly affected as we share comfort and encouragement with our fellow Christians, which is why the psalmist exclaims, "As for the saints in the land, they are the excellent ones, in whom is all my delight" (Ps. 16:3).

Every moment of our meeting together—singing songs of praise to God, listening to the preached Word, and encouraging one another—is designed to revive our affections for Christ. So, at the very mention of church, we should feel as David did: "I was glad when they said to me, 'Let us go to the house of the LORD!'" (Ps. 122:1).

GOD'S GOOD GIFTS

God not only gives us Scripture, prayer, and the refreshing shelter of his church to sustain Christlike emotions, he punctuates our whole lives with gracious gifts that enliven our feelings. Whether it is the chubby arms of a toddler wrapped around you in a hug, the taste of a popsicle on a hot day, a beautiful sunset, a crackling fire, the pungent smell of garlic, the sweet fragrance of a gardenia, the unexpected kindness of an encouraging word, the lavish goodness of a full pantry, the pleasure of a new dress, the thrill of a good book, or the blessings of companionship, God's gifts of beauty and pleasure are, as CJ puts it, like Post-it notes scattered throughout our daily lives, reminding us of the goodness and glory of God.[17]

"Every good gift and every perfect gift is from above, coming down from the Father of lights, with whom there is no variation or shadow due to change," James tells us (1:17). And because every good gift comes from God, every good gift is intended to direct our emotions back to God. "Pleasure," says Packer, is "divinely designed to raise our sense of God's goodness, deepen our gratitude to him, and strengthen our hope as Christians looking forward to the richer pleasures in the world to come."[18] Good gifts, rightly received, bolster our faith in the goodness of God and magnify the glorious worth of God—creating fresh affection and joy in our hearts.

Our challenge is to recognize God's good gifts. So often, we feel weighed down and depressed for this very reason: we fail to notice and appreciate the many wonderful gifts coming down from our generous God. But to cultivate the Christlike emotions we long for, we must cultivate a moment-by-moment awareness of God's good gifts. Admittedly, in the midst of suffering, this may seem almost impossible. At times the darkness of our lives seems unbroken by even the smallest flicker of goodness. But, even in our difficulties, God's gifts keep coming down. When we focus our gaze on his goodness, instead of our troubles, we can receive fresh infusions of hope.

Our friend from the previous chapter, the one with the difficult son, has learned to see how God intersperses good gifts throughout difficult days. "My son can be very disobedient one moment and very funny the next," she told us. "I have come to appreciate the funny things he says and does as gifts from God. When my son makes me laugh, it reminds me that God is with me, that he is helping me to persevere in training my son." Laughter, in the midst of a long day of mothering, is a Post-it note, a little reminder of God's goodness that lifts our discouraged emotions.

Even in the most horrific situations, God's good gifts can sustain our emotions. When Corrie Ten Boom and her sister,

Betsy, were imprisoned in Ravensbruck concentration camp, they smuggled in a small Bible on a string around Corrie's neck. Each night, women in their barracks would gather to read the Bible and pray. Not once did the guards disturb them, because the place was crawling with fleas. And so Corrie and Betsy gave thanks for the most unlikely of good gifts: the fleas that bit them mercilessly but also kept the guards away. God sends his good gifts into the lowest depths of human suffering. We can be cheered, if only we have eyes to see.

James not only tells us that "every good gift and every perfect gift is from above," he also reminds us of the greatest gift of all: salvation through God's Son. "Of his own will he brought us forth by the word of truth, that we should be a kind of firstfruits of his creatures" (James 1:17–18). CJ explains:

> James draws our attention to the preeminent display of God's goodness and generosity in the life of a Christian. Having created the universe, he does the unthinkable. He saves sinners who are deserving of his righteous wrath because of their sin. God's goodness and generosity are on display in his creative work, but even more in his redemptive work. This good and perfect gift cannot be improved upon.[19]

Every one of God's good and perfect gifts, and his salvation most of all, can be a means of grace to lift our downcast hearts, refresh our tired souls, and create new, Christlike emotions in our lives.

The Marvel of Emotional Maturity

What a gracious and glorious purpose God has for our feelings. This book is a small ladle—a teaspoon, really—dipped into the clear stream of God's Word on emotions, but we hope that these sips of truth will nourish your soul. We pray that you are more grateful than ever for the gift of your feelings, and full of faith for God's renewing work to make your emotions more like the beautiful and holy emotions of his Son.

Emotions give us the gift of insight. They *tell*. They report on the contours of our world, the sharp turns of trouble and adversity and the vibrant vistas of blessing and beauty. They make us perceptive to what pleases or pains another person, and—most wondrous of all—they enable us to more fully know and experience the immense love, boundless joy, stunning sovereignty, and glorious wisdom of our God. And emotions tell us how we are doing with God. Our affections for Christ show forth his miraculous work of grace in our souls; our unpleasant feelings are often the first to alert us that we have swallowed a lie or that a good value has turned bad.

Feelings can reveal our true condition—where we have veered from Scripture's straightedge or what has lured our attention from the supreme value of Christ—and stir us to turn back to the truth of God's Word. Our redeemed emotions shine a light down the gracious path of repentance. God gave us emotions to tell us when we've strayed so that we can return to him, and there is no greater gift than that.

Emotions also give us the gift of momentum. Christlike emotions can *move* us away from the edge of the cliff of sin and toward the green pastures of delight in God. Author Maurice Roberts writes:

> Ecstasy and delight are essential to the believer's soul and they promote sanctification. We were not meant to live without spiritual exhilaration, and the Christian who goes for a long time without the experience of heart-warming will soon find himself tempted to have his emotions satisfied from earthly things and not, as he ought, from the Spirit of God. . . . The believer is in spiritual danger if he allows himself to go for any length of time without tasting the love of Christ and savoring the felt comforts of a Savior's presence.[20]

Emotions are not dangerous. We are in danger, though, if our emotions are not satisfied in Christ. Godly feelings are a powerful defense against sin, moving us away from the heat of temptation; but they go on the offense as well, driving us "further up and further in" toward the glories of Christ.[21]

"If you love me, you will keep my commandments," declared our Savior (John 14:15). The crowning emotion of love, says Piper, "comes before and enables."[22] Feelings of love drive us to acts of self-sacrifice. Hatred of sin ignites repentance. Compassion compels kindness. Righteous anger catapults us to feats of courage. The hope of heaven thrusts us forward like a large, impervious ship, over the crashing waves of hardship in our lives. Thankfulness for our Savior's death and resurrection moves us to worship and praise. Christlike emotions empower a life of godliness.

Our emotional journeys have a glorious end. We can be full of hope and expectation now because a day is coming when our emotions will be forever changed. One day, we will feel no more heartache and heartbreak, for all our tears shall be wiped away (Rev. 21:4). One day, we will have no more sinful emotions, and every emotion we feel will be perfectly pleasing to God. On that day, our emotions will be like Christ's emotions, for "when he appears we shall be like him, because we shall see him as he is" (1 John 3:2).

Notes

Introduction: The Soaring Pays for the Thud . . . Or Does It?

1. L. M. Montgomery, *Anne of Avonlea* (New York: Bantam, 1988), 148–49.
2. While *feelings* and *emotions* are defined somewhat differently, they are often used synonymously in common language, which is what we will do in this book.

Chapter 1: Fact, Fiction, and Feelings

1. Helen Russell, "A Week Off from Facebook? Participants in Danish Experiment Like This," *theguardian.com*, November 10, 2015, http://www.theguardian.com/media/2015/nov/10/week-off-facebook -denmark-likes-this-happiness-friends?CMP=fb_gu.
2. Martyn Lloyd-Jones, *Spiritual Depression: Its Causes and Cure* (Grand Rapids, MI: Eerdmans, 1965), 109.
3. Charles Spurgeon, "Comfort for the Tempted," The Spurgeon Archive, accessed April 9, 2016, http://www.spurgeon.org/sermons/2603.php.
4. "Elisabeth Elliot Memorial Service at Wheaton College," YouTube video, July 31, 2015, https://www.youtube.com/watch?v=WSi3mR9 GQIE. This is a recording of the July 26, 2015, service. See especially 2:07.
5. Sam Williams, "Toward a Theology of Emotion," *Southern Baptist Journal of Theology* 7, no. 4 (2003): 59.
6. Brian Borgman, *Feelings and Faith: Cultivating Godly Emotions in the Christian Life* (Wheaton, IL: Crossway, 2009), 21–22.

Chapter 2: The Gift of Emotions

1. Edward T. Welch, *Side by Side: Walking with Others in Wisdom and Love* (Wheaton, IL: Crossway, 2015), 24.

2. *Baker Dictionary of Theology*, quoted in Brian Borgman, "Biblical Emotions: Biblical Foundations, Part 1" (sermon, Grace Community Church, Minden, NV, December 8, 2002), http://www.sermonaudio.com/playpopup.asp?SID=260416268.

3. Brian Borgman, "Biblical Emotions: Biblical Foundations, Part 2" (sermon, Grace Community Church, Minden, NV, December 15, 2002), http://www.sermonaudio.com/sermoninfo.asp?SID=260416282.

4. Os Guinness, *God in the Dark: The Assurance of Faith Beyond a Shadow of Doubt* (Wheaton, IL: Crossway, 1996), 127.

5. John M. Frame, *The Doctrine of the Knowledge of God* (Phillipsburg, NJ: P&R, 1987), 336.

6. Matthew Elliott, *Feel: The Power of Listening to Your Heart* (Carol Stream, IL: Tyndale, 2008), 14.

7. A. W. Tozer, *That Incredible Christian* (Harrisburg, PA: Christian Publications, 1986), loc 599.

8. D. G. Benner, "Emotion," in *Evangelical Dictionary of Theology*, 2nd ed., ed. Walter A. Elwell (Grand Rapids, MI: Baker Academic, 2001), 375.

9. Bruce and Jodi Ware, foreword to Brian Borgman, *Feelings and Faith: Cultivating Godly Emotions in the Christian Life* (Wheaton, IL: Crossway, 2009), 9.

10. John M. Frame, *Worship in Spirit and Truth* (Phillipsburg, NJ: P&R, 1996), 78.

11. Martyn Lloyd-Jones, *Spiritual Depression: Its Causes and Cure* (Grand Rapids, MI: Eerdmans, 1965), 52.

12. Jane Austen, *Sense and Sensibility* (New York: Knopf, 1992), 20.

13. Ibid., 177.

14. Lloyd-Jones, *Spiritual Depression*, 60.

15. Benner, *Evangelical Dictionary of Theology*, 375.

16. Antonio R. Damasio, *Descartes' Error: Emotion, Reason and the Human Brain* (New York: Grosset/Putnam, 1994), 130, 160.

Chapter 3: Why Do I Feel This Way?

1. Matthew Elliott, *Faithful Feelings: Rethinking Emotion in the New Testament* (Grand Rapids, MI: Kregel, 2006), 42.

2. Robert C. Solomon, *Not Passion's Slave: Emotions and Choice* (Oxford: Oxford University Press, 2003), 14.

3. Elliott, *Faithful Feelings*, 37.

4. "Other Quotations," The American Chesterton Society, accessed May 2, 2016, http://www.chesterton.org/other-quotations/. According to The American Chesterton Society, this quote originates with French playwright Jacques Duval.

5. John M. Frame, *The Doctrine of the Knowledge of God* (Phillipsburg, NJ: P&R, 1987), 336.

6. John Piper, quoted in Justin Taylor, "Tozer's Contradiction and His Approach to Piety," The Gospel Coalition, June 8, 2008, https://blogs .thegospelcoalition.org/justintaylor/2008/06/08/tozers-contradiction -and-his-approach_08/.

7. D. G. Benner, "Emotion," in *Evangelical Dictionary of Theology*, 2nd ed., ed. Walter A. Elwell (Grand Rapids, MI: Baker Academic, 2001), 375.

8. Os Guinness, *God in the Dark: The Assurance of Faith Beyond a Shadow of Doubt* (Wheaton, IL: Crossway, 1996), 128.

9. Robert W. Kellemen, "Emotional Intelligence: The ABC's of Emotions, Part 2: Why We Feel What We Feel," RPM Ministries, March 1, 2011, http://www.rpmministries.org/2011/03/why-we-feel-what-we-feel/.

10. Alasdair Groves, "What Do I Do with My Emotions? Engaging Your Emotions," The National CCEF Conference 2016 (conference session, October 15, 2016), https://www.ccef.org/shop/product/feelings -engaging-emotions.

11. L. M. Montgomery, *Anne of Avonlea* (New York: Bantam, 1998), 131.

12. Timothy Keller, *Walking with God through Pain and Suffering* (New York: Dutton, 2013), 215–16.

13. Groves, "Why Do I Feel How I Feel? Understanding Your Emotions," The National CCEF Conference 2016 (conference session, October 14, 2016), https://www.ccef.org/shop/product/feel-feel-understanding -emotions.

14. Ed Welch, *The Counselor's Guide to the Brain and Its Disorders*, rev. ed. (Glenside, PA: CCEF, 2015), 19.

Chapter 4: Feeling Good

1. Martin Luther and Wilhelm Pauck, *Luther: Lectures on Romans* (Louisville: Westminster John Knox Press, 2006), 159.

2. Timothy Keller, *Walking with God through Pain and Suffering* (New York: Dutton, 2013), 187.

3. John Piper, *Desiring God: Meditations of a Christian Hedonist*, 25th anniversary reference ed. (Colorado Springs: Multnomah, 2011), 117.

4. B. B. Warfield, "The Emotional Life of Our Lord," Monergism, accessed August 10, 2016, https://www.monergism.com/thethreshold /articles/onsite/emotionallife.html.

5. Clifford Pond, *The Beauty of Jesus: A Portrait of the Perfect Human Character of Jesus Christ and Some Applications to the Christian Life* (London: Grace Publications Trust, 1994), 92.

6. Mark Talbot, "Godly Emotions: Religious Affections, Expositions of Edwards's Major Works," desiringgod.org, September 1, 2004, http://www.desiringgod.org/articles/godly-emotions.

7. Ibid.

8. John Piper, *When I Don't Desire God: How to Fight for Joy* (Wheaton, IL: Crossway, 2013), 16.

9. A paraphrase of Augustine, *Confessions* 10.39 in Thomas R. Schreiner and Ardel B. Caneday, *The Race Set before Us: A Biblical Theology of Perseverance & Assurance* (Downers Grove, IL: InterVarsity Press, 2001), 17.

Chapter 5: Emotional Emergency Measures

1. Os Guinness, *God in the Dark: The Assurance of Faith Beyond a Shadow of Doubt* (Wheaton, IL: Crossway, 1996), 126, 128.

2. Elisabeth Elliot, "What to Do About Feelings," *The Elisabeth Elliot Newsletter*, January/February 2001, http://www.elisabethelliot.org/newsletters/2001-01-02.pdf.

3. David Pugmire, *Rediscovering Emotion* (Edinburgh: Edinburgh University Press, 1998), 129.

4. Elisabeth Elliot, *Discipline: The Glad Surrender* (Grand Rapids, MI: Revell, 2006), 142.

5. Guinness, *God in the Dark*, 126.

6. J. C. Ryle, *Matthew*, The Crossway Classic Commentaries (Wheaton, IL: Crossway, 1993), 261.

7. Ed Welch, *The Counselor's Guide to the Brain and Its Disorders,* rev. ed. (Glenside, PA: CCEF, 2015), 19.

8. Ibid., 19.

9. Ibid., 25.

10. John Piper, *When the Darkness Will Not Lift: Doing What We Can While We Wait for God—and Joy* (Wheaton, IL: Crossway, 2006), 25.

Chapter 6: How Do I Control My Emotions?

1. David Powlison, *Seeing with New Eyes: Counseling and the Human Condition through the Lens of Scripture* (Phillipsburg, NJ: P&R, 2003), 132.

2. Elisabeth Elliot, quoted in Tyler Smith, "In Memory of Elisabeth Elliot: 30 of Her Most Inspiring Quotes," *LogosTalk* (blog), June 15, 2015, https://blog.logos.com/2015/06/in-memory-of-elisabeth-elliot-30-of-her-most-inspiring-quotes/.

3. Martin Luther and Wilhelm Pauck, *Luther: Lectures on Romans* (Louisville: Westminster John Knox Press, 2006), 159.

4. John Piper, *For Your Joy* (Minneapolis: Desiring God, 2005), 39.

5. John Newton, *The Works of John Newton*, vol. 2 (Edinburgh: Banner of Truth, 2015), 7.

Chapter 7: Act to Feel

1. David Powlison, *Seeing with New Eyes: Counseling and the Human Condition through the Lens of Scripture* (Phillipsburg, NJ: P&R, 2003), 218.
2. Justin Taylor, "You Are What You Love: A Conversation with James K. A. Smith," The Gospel Coalition, April 6, 2016, https://blogs.the gospelcoalition.org/justintaylor/2016/04/05/you-are-what-you-love-a -conversation-with-james-k-a-smith/.
3. David Powlison, *Seeing with New Eyes: Counseling and the Human Condition through the Lens of Scripture* (Phillipsburg, NJ: P&R, 2003), 222.
4. C. H. Spurgeon, *The Treasury of David*, vol. 2 (McLean, VA: Macdonald, 1900), 51.
5. Dale Ralph Davis, *I Samuel: Looking on the Heart* (Fearn, Ross-shire, Scotland: Christian Focus, 2007), 18.
6. Robert Campbell Roberts, *Spiritual Emotions: A Psychology of Christian Virtues* (Grand Rapids, MI: Eerdmans, 2007), 27.
7. Mike Emlet, "Taste and See: Cultivating Godly Desires and Emotions," The National CCEF Conference 2016 (conference session, October 14, 2016), https://www.ccef.org/shop/product/taste-see-cultivating-godly -desires-emotions.
8. George Lewis Prentiss, *More Love to Thee: The Life and Letters of Elizabeth Prentiss* (Amityville, NY: Calvary Press, 1994), 420.

Chapter 8: God's Purpose in Pain

1. Dan B. Allender and Tremper Longman III, *The Cry of the Soul: How Our Emotions Reveal Our Deepest Questions about God* (Colorado Springs: NavPress, 1994), 14, 21.
2. David Powlison, *Seeing with New Eyes: Counseling and the Human Condition through the Lens of Scripture* (Phillipsburg, NJ: P&R, 2003), 222.
3. Charles Spurgeon, "The Cause and Cure of a Wounded Spirit," Sovereign Grace Audio Treasures, accessed April 9, 2016, http://www.sg -audiotreasures.org/spurgproverbs/spurgeon18-14.html.
4. Timothy Keller, *Walking with God through Pain and Suffering* (New York: Dutton, 2013), 241–42.
5. Martyn Lloyd-Jones, *Spiritual Depression: Its Causes and Cure* (Grand Rapids, MI: Eerdmans, 1965), 221.

6. Mark Talbot, "Godly Emotions: Religious Affections, Expositions of Edwards's Major Works," desiringgod.org, September 1, 2004, http://www.desiringgod.org/articles/godly-emotions.

7. C. S. Lewis, *The Problem of Pain* (San Francisco: HarperSanFrancisco, 2001), 92.

8. David Powlison, "God's Grace and Your Sufferings" in *Suffering and the Sovereignty of God*, eds. John Piper and Justin Taylor (Wheaton, IL: Crossway, 2006), 161.

9. Joni Eareckson Tada, "A Purpose in the Pain: An Interview with Joni Eareckson Tada," Ligonier Ministries website, October 1, 2011, http://www.ligonier.org/learn/articles/a-purpose-in-the-pain-an-interview-with-joni-eareckson-tada/.

10. Keller, *Walking with God through Pain and Suffering*, 247.

11. Christopher Ash, *Job: The Wisdom of the Cross* (Wheaton, IL: Crossway, 2014), 22.

12. Brian Borgman, *Feelings and Faith: Cultivating Godly Emotions in the Christian Life* (Wheaton, IL: Crossway, 2009), 90.

13. Keller, *Walking with God through Pain and Suffering*, 246.

14. Ibid., 253.

15. Charles Spurgeon, "Morning, August 31," Christian Classics Ethereal Library, accessed May 2, 2016, http://www.ccel.org/ccel/spurgeon/morneve.august.d0831am.html?highlight=august,31#highlight.

Chapter 9: Godly Emotions for Life

1. J. R. R. Tolkien, *The Return of the King* (New York: Ballantine Books, 2012), 17.

2. Ralph C. Wood, *The Gospel according to Tolkien: Visions of the Kingdom in Middle-Earth* (Louisville, KY: Westminster John Knox Press, 2003), 18; quoted in Justin Taylor, "Sad but Not Unhappy," The Gospel Coalition, August 19, 2010, https://blogs.thegospelcoalition.org/justintaylor/2010/08/19/sad-but-not-unhappy/.

3. J. R. R. Tolkien, *The Two Towers* (New York: Ballantine Books, 2012), 92.

4. Clifford Pond, *The Beauty of Jesus: A Portrait of the Perfect Human Character of Jesus Christ and Some Applications to the Christian Life* (London: Grace Publications Trust, 1994), 96.

5. B. B. Warfield, "The Emotional Life of Our Lord," Monergism, accessed August 10, 2016, https://www.monergism.com/thethreshold/articles/onsite/emotionallife.html.

6. John Piper, *Reading the Bible Supernaturally* (Wheaton, IL: Crossway, 2017), 104.

7. George Mueller, *A Narrative of Some of the Lord's Dealings with George Müller, Written by Himself, Jehovah Magnified. Addresses by George Müller Complete and Unabridged*, 2 vols. (Muskegon, MI: Dust and Ashes, 2003), 2:834, quoted in John Piper, *When I Don't Desire God: How to Fight for Joy* (Wheaton, IL: Crossway, 2013), 118.

8. Martyn Lloyd-Jones, *Spiritual Depression: Its Causes and Cure* (Grand Rapids, MI: Eerdmans, 1965), 61.

9. Brian Borgman, *Feelings and Faith: Cultivating Godly Emotions in the Christian Life* (Wheaton, IL: Crossway, 2009), 199.

10. George Mueller, "Soul Nourishment First," *The Baptist* 1, no. 3 (February 14, 1920).

11. R. C. Sproul, *The Prayer of the Lord* (Orlando, FL: Reformation Trust, 2009), 14.

12. Warren W. Wiersbe, *Real Worship: Playground, Battleground, or Holy Ground?*, 2nd ed. (Grand Rapids, MI: Baker, 2000), 22.

13. Jonathan Edwards, *The Works of Jonathan Edwards*, 2 vols. (Peabody, MA: Hendrickson, 1998), 1:242.

14. Martyn Lloyd-Jones and Kevin DeYoung, *Preaching and Preachers* (Grand Rapids, MI: Zondervan, 2011), 108.

15. Edwards, *Works*, 1:242.

16. J. I. Packer, *God's Words: Studies of Key Bible Themes* (Grand Rapids, MI: InterVarsity Press, 1981), 196.

17. CJ Mahaney, "Leisure" (sermon, Sovereign Grace Church, Louisville, KY, August 28, 2016), http://www.sgclouisville.org/sovereign-grace -church-louisville-sermons/sermon/2016-08-28/leisure-c-j-mahaney -genesis-2:1-3.

18. Leland Ryken, *J. I. Packer: An Evangelical Life* (Wheaton, IL: Crossway, 2015), 208.

19. CJ Mahaney, "Trials, Temptations, and Good Gifts" (sermon, February 21, 2016), http://www.sgclouisville.org/sovereign-grace-church -louisville-sermons/sermon/2016-02-21/trials-temptations-and-good -gifts-c-j-mahaney-james-1:13-18.

20. Maurice Roberts, *The Thought of God* (Edinburgh: Banner of Truth Trust, 1993), 57–58.

21. C. S. Lewis, *The Last Battle*, The Chronicles of Narnia (New York: HarperTrophy, 2005), 222.

22. John Piper, "The God Who Commands Our Emotions," desiringgod. org, August 12, 2015, http://www.desiringgod.org/interviews/the-god -who-commands-our-emotions.

General Index

Scripture Index

Also Available from
Carolyn Mahaney & Nicole Whitacre

For more information, visit crossway.org.